MT. SHASTA ASCENDED MASTER TEACHING

"And Ye shall know the Truth
and the Truth shall make
you free." John 8:32

By Nola Van Valer

Second Printing

P.O. Box 378
Mt. Shasta, CA 96067

ISBN - 0- 9641571-1-X

Tribute To Nola Van Valer

In 1930, Nola Van Valer, along with her husband Jerrett and several others met the Ascended Masters, face to face, on the slopes of Mt. Shasta. During the next ten years, for a month each summer, Nola traveled from her home in San Jose, California to Mt. Shasta, CA to be taught and trained in the work she would do for the Masters. She was invited into the Radiant Temple once each year during that time. Nola became an instrument for the Ascended Masters so they would have a vehicle for direct communication to bring Truth on earth. Because of her willingness to serve, the teachings that came forth spread throughout the United States and to many foreign countries.

In 1961, Nola moved permanently to Mt. Shasta. With a group of faithful students, she opened The Radiant School for Seekers and Servers in 1962. Through her tireless dedication to the Masters and their teachings she left behind a legacy that continues to help others expand their minds and lives with more purpose, understanding and truth.

Nola completed her earthly sojourn in 1979. The Radiant School was closed in 1984. The Truth lives on, woven into the fibers of many souls who were, and still are, touched by this work and the Masters who brought it forth.

The story of Nola's early encounters with the Masters on the slopes of Mt. Shasta is included in her earlier book, *My Meeting With The Masters On Mount Shasta.**

* *My Meeting With The Masters On Mount Shasta,* by Nola Van Valer, 1982, reprinted 1994. Published by Seekers and Servers, Mt. Shasta, CA 96067.

Introduction

Mt. Shasta is known and revered as a holy mountain throughout the world. The work in the Temples of the sacred mountains upon the earth affect the evolution and soul development of mankind. Each Temple has its particular work to do, and a council of Masters who direct it.

There are twelve Sons of God from the Melchizedek Order who comprise the Council of the Radiant Temple of Mt. Shasta. These are the Masters who worked with Nola Van Valer.

Phylos, known commonly to the world as Phylos, the Tibetan, author of *A Dweller On Two Planets** was the Ascended Master who was Nola's primary contact. After Nola and Jerrett met the Masters face to face in 1930, Nola began her work as an instrument for them to teach Truth to the world.

This book is a compilation of several aspects of the work of The Radiant School throughout the years. The first section is taken from the Friendly Letter Service. These letters were sent out to the students before the actual lessons began. The next section is from Yessue Ben Miriam, known as Jesus Christ. This section is primarily about thinking as it relates to body function, health and spiritual expansion. The next portion is from discourses given by the Ascended Masters and study lessons of The Radiant School

The teachings of Phylos and the council were designed to help man expand his thinking. Using the mental mind to reach beyond the visible realms, man is drawn into the higher divisions of Mind and to the higher worlds. These teachings help draw man upward to his own process of completion and ascension from earthly life.

Knowledge of the Truth of what man is, how he is made, and the divine potential within him, breaks the bonds of ignorance and fear. When Truth is lived, it produces love and reverence for God that promotes a joyous desire for service to all life. Truth is the power that brings unity of God and man, as God in man. "Know the Truth and the Truth will set you free."

It is with heartfelt gratitude to God, the Ascended Masters, Nola, and to all the seekers and servers through the years who have made it possible to bring *Mt. Shasta Ascended Master Teaching* to print. May the blessing of the Ascended Masters be upon you as you read.

* *A Dweller On Two Planets,* by Phylos, written by Fredrick S. Oliver, 1894. Reprinted by Borden Publishing Company

TABLE OF CONTENTS

CHARTS

Love Law

Love is that portion of God that I can use. It enters into my mind and body and I this self must express it. I shall be at peace with love as I meet all my fellowmen. In every part of work I do it shall be love and at the end of the day I shall have that portion of love that is my share. It shall quench my thirst and shall still the beating of my heart until I am one with God.

Amen. Amen. Amen.

1

THE SEEKER AND SERVER

A seeker is one who is not satisfied with a purely materialistic life, good as that may be. Surely there is more to life than business, eating, and sleeping. So the seeker sets out on the long path to find his birthright, and the reasons for being a mortal man on earth.

Because there are seekers in the world, this would tend to verify the fact that there is something to find. Scientists have said we cannot know without experiencing, and this has the ring of Truth. They put limits on this idea however, by saying we must experience in this lifetime, which is not necessarily true. If experience is essential to knowledge, then seekers, by this very definition, are looking for something they once had through experience, but lost. This is further borne out by the feeling of joyous recognition when they do find something in the beauty of the eternal.

This search is for spiritual Truth. There are many students who want knowledge, but they are not true seekers until they include the eternal verities in their search. Spiritual facts, not being material, are not subject to proof in the material world. Therefore, what is proof of a spiritual Truth to one man will not be proof to another. This is why science has very little success in proving or disproving religious claims. The scientific method is applied on a different level than the one seekers contact to learn of Spirit.

The reasoning power of your mind is to be used in seeking understanding of the greatest mysteries of life. Do, by all means, test what you are told, or what you read, by your own standards of Truth. You are the judge, and your experiences in life constitute an inner jury. On each basic idea, the seeker finds this judge and jury will bring in a verdict of true, false, possible, or judgment reserved. It is only as you progress in your understanding that you see the ramifications of Truth, develop the mental power to grasp a myriad of details, and fit them into their proper places in your pattern of life.

When, at last you arrive at those higher levels of the spiritual world, you will find what was true here on earth is still true, but you are different. You will bring to that Truth a greater understanding, see where it has higher application, and how one Truth blends perfectly with another. Truth is simple; beware of teachings that omit this priceless quality.

Does the idea of other lives and other experiences disturb you? Christian teachings include the idea of a life after the death of your body. Did this ever strike you as a one-sided affair, similar to a stick with only one end? Eternal life would embrace both ends of the stick; both ends of mortal life on earth. To accept the idea of pre-existence in spirit before birth into this world, should make it possible for you to envision other lives in flesh. If God wants his human children to grow to spiritual maturity and become perfect, and Jesus has assured you that He does, how else are you going to do it? One lifetime is like a drop of water in the ocean, or a grain of sand on the beach.

Once you start this blessed search, never stop! What else could hold such a vital interest? We will quote John Milton, "Truth is compared in Scriptures to a streaming fountain; if her waters flow not in perpetual progression, they sink into the muddy pool of conformity and tradition."

There is an ancient question that, even today, people are asking themselves: "Am I my brother's keeper?" You are your brother's keeper in the sense that you should care what becomes of him, and you should let him know this. There is far too much indifference about the fate of millions of people in this world, many of whom are living lives of quiet desperation.

The best kind of help to offer first to anyone is understanding. An impartial, friendly interest in his welfare, cannot fail to have a good effect on his morale. Second, the aid you offer him should enable him to help himself. This cannot be stressed too strongly, or too often. An independent man is a functioning unit, a going concern. He has pride. He can have integrity, and he can afford to be concerned about the welfare of others. So you see in answering the first question, we come to full circle.

The other side of the coin of service is you as the server. When a server is mentioned, one immediately thinks of a servant. In a way this is true. A server is a servant, but to serve one's fellowman does not mean to be servile, nor a doormat. A servant's position seems to be a humble one, but is it? Jesus said, "The last shall be the first and the first shall be the last." If Jesus did not despise the menial tasks that were helpful to others, who are you to do so? It does not matter to God whether you lead the parade of humanity, or bring up the rear; it is your motive in doing so that is important.

There is a great difference between an officious person deciding what is "best" for someone else, and a simple willingness to do the task at hand, pleasant or not, with cheerfulness and a smile. The qualities of willingness and good humor are worth at least as much as the service. Who likes to have grudging service? Ah, but what a joy it is to be served by one who has a song in their heart.

Suppose one diligently seeks for Truth over the years and finds it. His life can be filled with the beautiful light of this Truth, and his joy can grow to such proportions that he must share it with someone else or burst. He is impelled to say, "I have found the light, come and see it with me." For if a man has Truth and shares it not, he has lost it in the beginning. It is in brief moments of great illuminating joy, that you are closest to the doorway of Heaven.

The most wonderful way a server can give to a fellowman is to help him to a better understanding of himself and his world, to lift his spirit on wings of inspiration, and to offer him a philosophy of life in which hope is enthroned. The giving of wealth was not the riches meant in giving unto others. Rich beyond measurement are the qualities of mind that bring untold joy to the hearts of men.

Allow each man to live his own life and die his own death. Do not sympathize with his hurt, rather have mercy for those who are willing to bring everything to the altar, as it pleases God. They are the ones who need your mercy and condolence to help them face the grief and to learn self-sacrifice. Unless you distinguish between the worthy and unworthy, you make no progress, for those most in need of helping themselves, will ask the most of you.

There are hazards in service. You must learn to wait until asked to render aid. You must learn to give and to serve with wisdom. As each one learns to consult the silence within himself, he will gradually become aware of the true need of the one he would serve. When your attention is centered on Christ, and you are open to the lead of the God within, you will never go astray in the use of any of your gifts.

2

THE OVERCOMER

Only a tiny bit of God has come to earth with each of you. That infinitesimal grain is nevertheless sufficient to help you see through the difficulties and problems of life, and to overcome them so that you can rise to your divine sonship. Each man has a higher and lower body. The higher ethereal body is composed of extremely fine particles and the lower is made of atoms of matter. He also has a higher and a lower mind: the higher is called the God Mind and the lower is the physical function of mortal man's thinking. The answers to most problems that plague mankind today lie between the physical nature of man and the spiritual source of man. When through experience, you can see the wisdom of putting aside your mortal concepts, then your own God Mind is free to use your physical body to express God's will on earth. This is another way of saying that such a person has attained their Christ consciousness.

It is said that it is well to keep the eye on the ball, the ear to the ground, and the shoulder to the wheel. Now try to work in that position! This ridiculous example will show you that a teaching given with one problem in mind, cannot always be applied to another because it will not fit. Life in the training of the intellect is marked by that which is high and low. There is great confusion among groups of people because what is given as great spiritual Truth to all, if you try to fit it to your thinking ability, does not always work. So when the great teacher, Jesus, was on earth and He found this difference in His groups, He always said, "Let us reason or think on these things."

So the student who aspires to higher spiritual teaching must first go as far as he can with his mortal understanding. He must be able to extend his seeking thoughts outward where they will touch ideas that do not come down close to the aura of the body. Ideas do not come into the physical world; they descend to the ethereal world, and the student must extend his thinking upward and away from the body in order to draw the idea into his first aura to be studied. This is how inventors and scientists bring new ideas into being in the physical world.

When a student begins serious study, he takes himself apart and sees all the many things which he has done and judges as wrong, or thinks have harmed someone else. He says, "I do not know when I am forgiven." When he begins to take his day apart and he hears, sees, or feels, the many places during his day where he has not been right and he is willing to face it, he will find not only forgiveness, but the ability to do things right. Many refer to this act as the Comforter, for it is through the compassion of Christ that love replaces doubt or fear in your life. The greatest problem a spiritual student has is admitting to himself that he is wrong. Once this barrier can be broken down, advancement of thinking students will indeed go on and on.

Spiritual discernment means tuning into the unlimited supply of God knowledge. This does not mean that the problems man meets on earth will be eliminated. The true meaning is that with every growth in human understanding, the God Mind is drawn into greater activity in the life, and the understanding is greater for every problem man has to meet. Everyone should stop and look carefully at his problems. It is through these problems that spiritual gains are made. Man's temptations are the exact thing needed to round out his spiritual education.

An alcoholic will have little success in overcoming his problem until he discovers the conviction within himself that he is the only master of his problems. He cannot do it by thinking it out one day and saying to himself, "I will", for the mortal will is weak. When he is capable of understanding that it is by the power of his God Will, then it can be done. So likewise it is with every problem: sickness, financial troubles, or obstruction of understanding. If you will take whatever you cannot solve before the Throne of God, submit your mortal will, and believe wholeheartedly that the God Will can do all things, only then have you stepped aside and allowed your Higher Self to deal with the problems.

What we are discussing is not so easily accomplished. If it were an easy problem that man is faced with, there would be no difficulty, nor would man have to return to earth over and over again to learn that which he has failed to grasp in his past incarnations. How many lives have been spent to learn the answer to one problem? We can say, "Many!" When some people are able to overcome sickness or to make manifestations of prosperity more or less quickly, it is not the first time they have met that problem. So you should not judge how quickly one person is making their manifestations or how slowly another is passing through the trials and tribulations of physical life.

Man still has the right to choose whether he shall make use of the God Power of overcoming or use his self will. God has prepared the way for each man's greatest unfoldment. If man approaches the problem and sees it with the eyes of God upon it, he can find the solution and never have that problem again. This does not mean that he will be free from problems, because he will have others come to perplex him. God sees each man in his unfoldment and judges his strength accordingly, with rest periods between, so that man is never taken beyond what he is able to do. God permits unfoldment according to the plan of each man's life.

People who are distressed by separation through death would not weep if they could see the great relief of those who come to the ethereal realms. When you learn the true meaning of death, you are then at the place where you use prayer for freedom. Great joy awaits those who come through what is called death, to the side of life you do not see, where they have no more pain, sorrow, or heartache, and thus ends the mortal will of comparison.

Not by the yard, quart, gallon, bushel, ton, nor by the weight of the carat does man receive according to his needs. Those who pray for wealth, even though they say, "just enough", have set a law within themselves, for they do not know what enough is. A man in financial difficulty needs to take his problem before his Throne of God and see it as a problem and not as a certain amount of money. When he can forget banks and offices where money is loaned, and turn within himself and bless the Heavenly Father for the physical supplies that have been furnished, then the spiritual can demonstrate and provide whatever is needed.

A man should take his problems singly into that Chamber of Silence where he comes face to face with his Higher Self and say, "Dear God, this is all I have. I bring it to Your Throne and I accept in return my freedom." He should not think of it further but let it rest there with his "Amen. Amen. Amen." If he can forget it, the answer will come before he realizes because God's supply is unlimited. It will fill every need. It is in giving that man receives. What man has endeavored to give, multiplies.

Any human being who accepts his heartaches, grief, pains, or lack of supply as a lesson, is never denied his freedom from these things. But first he must acknowledge that he needs that lesson. He needs to know that God works within him, not through others for him. Those who ask for freedom from their burdens should not expect anyone else to work out their problems for them. They should concentrate on their own thoughts as well as their acts. By concentration they will find purification, and eventually freedom from the collar that rubs, the yoke that pulls, and the burden that is so useless.

If man must see how spiritual illumination is given to him, his eyes will be forever closed. The understanding of mortal man is only of the laws of nature in three dimensions. The laws of the Spiritual Self which are in command over all the laws of nature belong only to the God Self, to which man must turn with acknowledgment in order to receive. Therefore, man in his mortal thinking says, "I think and reason this out." If his reasoning gets no higher than the third dimension, his physical senses rule. But if his Higher Self becomes the ruler in his life, it brings the working of the fourth dimension into being. He does not SEE the answer, he FEELS it, and feels within himself the joy of the rightness of wisdom that comes from God.

Man does not create Ideas, they are already created and exist in the ether around him. The Pattern or Idea of a hammer has already existed. When the stone age man first got the idea for a hammer, he drew the Thought pattern into his mind, and put it into action by making a hammer to use. So it is with all things. When you have expanded your thinking ability by use, it becomes a powerful magnet for Ideas and they are attracted to you like iron filings to a real magnet. By much concentrated thinking about what he seeks to find, a scientist will draw an Idea to himself from the ether. When he is finished with that Idea, it goes back out into space, and travels around the earth in every vibration that is there.

This is why inventions and discoveries have been made at about the same time by people in widely separated places. Nicola Tesla, called the prodigal genius, "saw" his inventions in mental imagery before he made them. He put very little down on paper but worked from his mental images. He would order parts made to specifications without having an overall blueprint. When they were assembled, they not only fit, they worked. Because of this method, however, many of the things he "thought out" were lost to the world because no record was left.

Language has nothing to do with Idea Patterns at all, for when Ideas are drawn into your minds, the education you have enables you to clothe them with your own words and thus understand what they mean. Mental application is concentrated work and the only way you digest the meaning of Ideas is by paying attention to them.

There are many who do not have a change of thought come into their lives for days, months, or sometimes for years. Others have become so aware of the things that have been created in the space about them, that they have no time to take one and look at it and think about it. They are mentally racing about undisciplined, knowing the existence of many ideas but unable to do anything about them, and so they accomplish nothing.

You will find sheep are mentioned in the Bible many times. They represent the thoughts of your physical mortal mind. When you wonder about God: where He is, what He does, how He knows what you are thinking, and how He can reach you, these thoughts cause you to reach out into the things you do not see. You reach into that which you cannot touch because it has no solid manifestation. When the "sheep" are sacrificed, it means you have reached a point in your spiritual development where you wish to give up your own mortal thinking in order to find enlightenment by turning to your Higher Self.

When Jesus is portrayed searching the mountain for the lost sheep, what is lost is the knowledge of how men make contact with their God Minds. Jesus represents your own state of consciousness; the sheep are the mortal thoughts; mountain means knowledge; and the fold is the Soul at rest with God. Now put this together and think what it means when Jesus finds the lost sheep on the mountain and returns them to the fold.

What then is Faith? Is it the substance of things hoped for, the evidence of things not seen? Faith is an essence from a higher realm. You draw it to you in the form of substance, which is attracted to you by the magnetic property of your Thoughts. This substance is actually a picture of what you believe. This picture materializes, in reality, in the physical world, when your faith is strong enough, and your thought is concentrated on a particular thing.

You can have anything you want, but not have everything you want. You believe in a thing because of what, to you, is adequate proof. When you have faith in that thing, it is without tangible evidence, and involves the functioning of the Higher Mind. When you do not have faith but want it, you must reach out into the Thought World and draw the substance of faith to you by your own desire. Serenity is part of faith, and you must be willing to allow what will be, to be. Seeking to learn more of the eternal Truths, and putting them into practice in your lives, will build faith.

If you could see into the World of Thoughts, or the

fourth dimension, you would see thought pictures floating all around you. They move around the surface of the aura smoothly, as if on ball bearings. This is why physical speech is not necessary in the Heavenly Worlds. In the heavenly worlds, everyone's aura is quite visible to others and it is impossible to conceal what one is thinking. It also helps to explain why communication between the higher realms and the physical world of mankind is sometimes difficult to accomplish accurately. Thought on the higher side of the veil is in picture symbols, while men of earth think in word symbols. Considerable translating by man is therefore necessary with the ever-present possibility of errors in receiving the intended meaning. People should be aware of this and guard against error by asking questions.

Why do most people have low periods when their faith ebbs away? Sometimes you use up more energy than you should. When the body is drained of energy, you have trouble reaching the God Mind or the Higher Self, through which faith functions. In this condition, you can be plagued by entities in the spirit world, and by injurious thinking like hate or anger that comes from other people. You are constantly being battered by other people's thinking.

It is well to ask God for protection from harmful thinking, knowing by faith it will be done. "Oh ye of little faith," Jesus said. When you feel this absence of faith, the best thing to do is seek inspiration through whatever stirs you the most. It may be music, the natural grandeur of the forest, or the solitude of the mountain that stirs you. The altitude of the mountain helps you meditate because you are above the currents of thinking on a low plane that hugs the lower lands.

Many times Jesus went up to the mountains to be alone. If you live in a crowded city and cannot visit forest or mountain, you can still be alone for meditation, but you must plan on it, and insist on it. Little by little you can build an inner core of peace that will enable you to be calm whatever occurs. The peacefulness generated in meditation will bless the rest of your day, and will enable you to think problems through to a more successful solution. Some people are satisfied with the Truth they already have, but when you seek to learn from your Higher Self, more profound Truth will come to you.

Sometimes people, especially young people say, "I believe in God, but I don't want to think about the spiritual world. I am in the physical world and I feel that I should live my physical life here and now. The spiritual life will come later." This is like trying to paint a picture when you are color blind, or groping through life in the dark when you could have the light to guide you all the way. The physical is produced by the spiritual, and controlled by it, in regard to pattern and Divine Laws. Your contribution in this framework provided by God, is your own free will decision to direct your life upward, or let it drift downward. Do you try to live according to your highest ideals, and by a perfect pattern guided by Divine Laws? Or do you live by what your neighbor, and the majority of mankind thinks is right?

The more you know about the spiritual world, the more you have to guide you in the physical world, and the more rapid progress you can make in the mastery of life. The purpose of life is to raise your awareness above the physical things of this world, into the continual awareness of God's Presence in all things. This does not derogate the physical body or physical life as many religious and esoteric teachings do, but indeed dignifies them by the knowledge that God is literally in everything.

Could you devise a better world system, in which a

myriad of beings could learn many and complex lessons? This is a wonderful world, all things considered. The things you don't like about it are the result of man's selfishness, greed, cruelty, and his breaking of Divine Laws; knowingly and unknowingly. It is not necessary to have strife, unhappiness, or ill health, to the extent that you do on earth. To change, you will only need to seek out the Divine Laws, which are perfectly knowable, and live according to the will of God.

If all of you who hear these words would find a few moments daily, or more often, when you may be motionless and silent, dismissing all earthly things from your mind, you would find your body rejuvenated and your strength returned. Man does not give his physical body enough time to relax, without being compelled to do something. It has little chance to take in fresh energies, even though the mind, which works much faster, is capable of going on.

It is the driving which wears out the body. In your busiest moments when you feel rushed beyond expression, if you will go by yourself and relax completely, sit down in quietness for as little as five minutes, you will never miss the time. You will be able to resume your work at full capacity. How far out into space can you see? If you cannot see the open sky and you cannot leave where you are, simply close your eyes and try to see into space, it will be the same. Just realize that only in the mortal world are you compelled by time. In God's Kingdom there is no time. The realization of this great Truth will enable you to feel less rushed, and thus accomplish more.

3

THE OPEN MIND

In the Bible's Book of Acts, Jesus is quoted as having said, "Until you break down the wall or partition between, and make of all one perfect whole, you can not enter the Kingdom of Heaven." What was the wall He was referring to? Do you place before any new experience of life, a wall of resistance, and determine not to accept anything unless you have already decided it is true? Do you place, perhaps, a wall of ignorance before yourself? This wall must be broken down in order to make yourself one perfect whole.

It is quite possible that a man who has fixed opinions is right, perhaps unknowingly right. Maybe he is aware of his rightness, but he must know how that rightness should be used, whether it is in the Divine or in the material way. If it is not used correctly, it will mean nothing. There are those who are afraid to learn, for fear they will have to give up what they already have decided is the only way. So beware of having too fixed an opinion, for it is much easier to learn with an open mind, than to give up something you believed was right but later discovered was not. A man who is willing to learn and does not have fixed opinions, will grasp the Truth so quickly that you would think he already knew it.

Some people, after completing their schooling believe they have learned to express what they are thinking through the use of words. Their thoughts, however, are mainly concerned with their own decisions, and their lives are run upon those decisions. Only when a man comes up against a problem that he cannot solve by his own thinking or decisions as judgments, will he find he must use more mind power than he has from his physical senses or common-sense thinking. These problems are the very ones he needs to unfold his dormant God-power, and make him realize that solutions do not come through education alone.

It is well to remember the dual nature of everything: positive and negative, hot and cold, pleasant or unpleasant, comfort as ease, and discomfort as disease. If you stand before a majestic statue that represents Truth, you form an opinion of what it is like. One who stands on the east will see it in a different light effect than one who stands on the west, and may come to entirely different conclusions and understanding. So, you may become confused by how you approach a thing to understand it in its fullness.

Are you fanatical about anything? It may apply to any part of life's expression: food, religion, dress, or choice of friends. Are you set against a new approach to learning? Are you a good listener? Many a man expounds his own thinking of what is good and not good, and fails to listen carefully to others to learn something. He may never know what his conversational partner has buried in the mine of his memory that may be fascinating to a listener. When, for instance, older people pass on, their many stirring experiences of a different world than you ever knew are gone forever with them. Fellowship will break down the wall between people. The warmth of friendship can expand one's perceptiveness, if one listens attentively. Each of you must be capable of reading, hearing, and seeing beyond what is said, to get the full Truth.

Every intelligent person should consider this point

well: one who is critical and cannot accept new ideas excludes himself from the universal program in his life. It behooves you all to witness improvement in yourselves first. The unity which is spoken of in the Bible excludes none and includes all, even those who do not think as you think. It should make no difference. Every man should be accepted as a human being, entitled to consideration by all other thinking personalities.

People generally are willing to be good, yet they do not change. They have mentally set the law of what they think goodness is. They think, "If I try to reach this goal and fail, I do not want anyone else to know it." They succeed in being what they consider good, yet they sometimes make the people around them uncomfortable through remarks that are not tactful.

A man should know when he is right. But it is also good to know what wrongfulness is because it shows him the opposite view and enables him to set his course correctly. There is the man who becomes a religious fanatic; he is one who says a thing is true even when he cannot believe it himself. Yet good reasoning ability and good power of mind will tell him that it cannot be that way. He becomes afraid of his own judgment for fear he will have to change his thinking. Therefore, to him there is but one road, one way, and he will declare he is on it. He will argue and make you listen to him, but he will not listen to you. He thunders and pounds, and claims the Bible will prove what he says, but he never proves he knows what the Bible means.

Many problems face the world today. People are trying to figure out which side they are on. Can they believe in the God power, or must they form their own ideals of self? If the mammon laws will give happiness, pleasure, and forgetfulness, then are they not better than the God power? The good man believes there is but one Being to take care of all the peoples of the earth, good or bad. The other believes that there is no God that equals the material opportunities of mammon. Here we have two decided opinions that are pitted against one another. The only answer is to be a willing listener. But if it becomes beyond what you can control in your emotions or feelings, walk away from it. If you are the one who has a set opinion, and if you are bound to make others believe that opinion, then live the life that proves it. Prove to your neighbors, family, and friends, that you are God-like and your ideas will need no explanation.

If you study the Ten Commandments you will find they are among the greatest parables in the Bible. "THOU SHALL HONOR THY FATHER AND MOTHER," literally speaking, man believes this refers to his physical parents. But it also means the Father-Mother within him, his Higher Self, his God-Self. When this idea is thought through, accepted, and put into action, all other things become stepping stones. "THOU SHALT NOT KILL" also means thou shalt not kill the life that came to fulfill your pattern, thou shalt not kill this opportunity. "THOU SHALT NOT STEAL": you certainly should not take what does not belong to you, but it also means thou shalt not push your personality, your individuality or your mind power on anyone else.

Again it said, "THOU SHALT NOT JUDGE." There are very few, if any, people who do not judge their fellowmen. When you judge a man for his acts, it is condemnation. If his acts are against the morals of men, he needs correction, not judgment or death. When you find a person you think is admirable, bless him because he is capable of living his life. Do not attempt to see behind his curtain. Whatever life you have, learn to form it of the best, not what some other person has found good, but according to your pattern. Life then becomes an opportunity of acceptance rather than a judgment. There is so much to learn about the Golden Rules.

Countless people need friends; non-critical, understanding, comradely neighbors. They may be friendless because they find it hard to hold friends or to make new ones. They should ask themselves a few questions, such as, "What have I found in my lifetime that is worth sharing? Do I hold only for myself, the good things I have found? Am I the secretive type?" If you have complete happiness, if you have pleasant surroundings, do you allow yourself to become self-satisfied or be filled with your own concerns?

Learn to share what you have of beauty, abundance, strength, and of mental and spiritual food. Learn to share with whomever comes into your home or into your presence, whether for a few moments, an hour or a day. Let them take away with them the fullness of what has satisfied you. You will find yourself reaching higher for what you do not have yet, in order to serve others better, knowing it is possible to find it. In possessing this new abundance, you can share again, and in that way you will grow daily. You will move away from your selfish aloneness and the carelessness of not spending enough time in your abundance to know its great value. Take stock of what you prize most, that is what you should share with others. What you prize most is what you have earned through experiences that never need to be repeated.

The troubles you experience in your life or home are the things you must surmount. Until you take each troublesome thing apart and study it from all angles, you cannot know how to overcome it. When you allow little troubles to remain without doing anything about them, they become increasingly difficult to overcome. If you will face each trouble as it comes into your life, you may find at the end of the day, the problem is no longer there or that a solution for it has been found.

Although you may feel that you cannot have more problems, with each one you overcome you open the door for a higher one. If you shy away from meeting what each day brings, you will find your life cluttered with annoyances, leaving little room for happiness or satisfaction, because there is little success. Then there is nothing you can share, because others do not want your troubles.

Too many people are trying to share their troubles instead of their good thoughts, deeds, services and possessions. They try to shove their troubles onto another person's shoulders because they are tired of carrying their own worldly burdens. We tell you, "Your troubles are your tests." If you will be aware each day that only by God's power working through YOU, will those tests dissolve and pass away, then you will find room for new things, and the way to the Higher Path. It does not run a straight line or a smooth course. It is ever upward and it is harder to climb each day and each year. The strength for the climb is gained through the overcoming of the lesser trials. Though the climb may get harder, it will seem less so, as one's spiritual muscles become accustomed to the exertion.

At the end of your life, if you have been able to reach the height where the path ends, you can look out over the plains of the lives that you have lived. Then you can see that only through the great Power that came to you from your Heavenly Father, did you overcome the trials, sins, and temptations that make up life on earth. When a sin or temptation comes, meet it! Do not run away from it, but seek the will to overcome it. In that way you are wiser, stronger, and your temptations become fewer. God can manifest in a stronger way through an overcomer than He can in those who do nothing to defeat their temptations.

There are some who decide that all teachings held out to them as Truth are very poor substance for them to think about. When a man feels that he is above what is being taught, he has failed to see that all things taught belong to him in their season. This does not mean that he must put these views into action in his own life. He will find through knowing how other people think, observing the rules they live by, or the obligations they accept as part of their lives, he can gain a greater understanding and a greater ability to guide his own course.

He must never permit himself to have frozen opinions, be self-righteous, or above all, to judge others from that self-righteous attitude. He should never believe that only one way, his way, can be the right way. If a man is a drunkard, that may be the way he must learn Truth, who is to say that he is wrong? He may not be eligible for certain society; he may not be a good companion; he may have given up rights to home and family and is not welcome there. However to deliberately judge him as an evil man, lost to the devil or Satan, doomed to hell, is not true. There are many examples of men who have risen to great service among their fellowmen after a period of life apparently lost in drunkenness.

When you come to the other side of death, you will see that you are responsible for the mistakes you made. Although they may be the same as some other person's mistakes, the results are not similar and the penalties are not the same. It is according to what you think: your own self-punishment is the judgment you have made on others. Therefore, those who find themselves in that plight when they arrive on the other side of life, in the place where they must undo their mistakes, will have no difficulty in knowing what benefit a certain action has brought them and what disadvantages it has caused in their lives.

No man on earth can say that his life is the perfect life, for even Jesus did not claim to be good. He said, "I AM the Way, the Truth and the Life." (John 14:6) He was not speaking of Himself or His personality. He was telling each man that his "I AM", his Christness, his spark of divinity was the way, the Truth, and the life for him. Whatever way it shines is the way it will lead you upward in consciousness. This is the deeper meaning of the words, "To thine own self be true." This is the self to which you should all be true, the highest part of you.

Words are useless things if the meaning behind them is not clear. Happy thoughts should be expressed in words that fit them. Words that do not give enlightenment or encouragement are not fit words for any happiness, joy, or test that has been made in your life. You must be willing to work to find the Truth. Look up in an unabridged Webster's dictionary the words used in the Bible, even words whose meanings seem obvious. Smaller dictionaries do not give enough information about derivative root meanings of words in use. Ask God to show you the true meaning of each word, and the parables that are as familiar to you as your own backyard will become like a foreign country and will reveal many things. The "I AM" that Jesus referred to had no personality, but is the unawakened Christ quality within each one of you. When it is in action, it is the Conscience in every man.

So, greet each new day with a resolve that you will do all that you can to awaken that "I AM" Christ consciousness within you. Allow yourself to move forward into greater awareness and, thereby, greater enjoyment of the wonderful potential for good that is within and about you everywhere. Let that potential become a living reality and your life will be filled with its blessings.

4

THE CROWN OF FRIENDSHIP

Man cannot live unto himself. Except in rare cases, little is gained either on earth or in heaven when man lives alone, seeing only his way of accomplishing his work on earth. Each man must realize he has something of value to do besides tending to himself. People come together as neighbors, friends, and family for a particular reason, so each may help the other learn life's lessons, so they may be free from this earth-bound body. Those who seek Truth, should understand that the people they mingle with every day are the ones God expects them to enlighten, when and where they can. How happy you are when someone is able to do this for you.

To learn the Truth of friendship, offer it to a stranger! When two people meet, opposite in nature, thinking and acting, they have a Heaven-sent opportunity for the greatest friendship, because one helps the other understand many things. How wonderful to have a friend who knows you! He knows when your privacy should not be disturbed, when he can drop in unannounced, when he should not repeat the things you tell him, and you know similar things about him. You can trust him to do the right thing. He permits you freedom of action and thought and you are able to be yourself in his company.

When you help a friend grow in spiritual stature, you are serving God. There is much confusion and misunderstanding among the people of the world because so many of them live in violation of the impersonal laws of the universe. There are laws of cause and effect that govern social relationships, as well as gravity, and they are just as inexorable. Countless people do not know that they are breaking these laws, which is the reason for many of their miseries. They just know something is badly out of adjustment in their lives.

If a friend appeals to you for counsel, tell him he can discover these natural laws for himself if he will sincerely seek them with no preconceived ideas. Those fortunate ones who live in constant awareness of the universal laws are blessed by harmony, usefulness, and joy, despite the fact that many of them have severe handicaps to overcome. They are the men and women of your world who command the highest respect and love from their fellowmen.

Friendship is needed everywhere. One trouble with your world today is that many people are trying to get what others have. With some, it is food or clothing; with others it is education, but in a great many places it is freedom. Those who have freedom should value it and share it with others. When you do not share friendship, you do not share freedom.

Friendship flourishes best in the free atmosphere that exists between equals. Perhaps there is something of far-reaching importance here. When men who are white, brown, black or yellow, meet on a basis of equality, then they can call each other friend. There are unseen differences between the races; indeed the outward differences of skin color are but an indication of this. Each race is learning specific lessons from life, and has something particular to itself to contribute to the culture of the world. When we understand this, the differences that before were puzzling and perhaps a source of irritation on both sides, become enlightened. Friendship is born as thoughts of understanding are born for one another. As individuals, we are drawn to people who are most like ourselves, since like seeks like. This does not mean likeness of outward characteristics, but inner ones. Friendship in its highest expression is a similarity of Soul qualities.

Now, one who sees all the faults in his friend may still be on the first rung of the ladder. One who has many faults may not even know he has reached a higher step because he does not consider himself superior. True friendship is the ability to see your friend's Higher Self, instead of the lower self where faults are grounded. Thinking they know right from wrong, and seeing the faults in their friends, many people decide to stay away from them. Is this a wise decision? There is good in everyone. Though they may commit the very evil you say is beyond your understanding, it may be through this lesson they reach their highest overcoming point, just as Paul, Judas, and Thomas did.

Be careful what you say to your friend for intention is what counts. Friendship is not nurtured in unkind remarks. Words will not kill but may hurt, injure, or hinder the growth of the Soul so much that a life could be wasted. It is better to walk away than to say something harmful if you intend it to be a barb. When you are displeased with yourself because you are unhappy about what you said or did, or because you had not been acting from your own Higher Self, you have the opportunity to correct the mistake. However, when you are not aware of it you are not capable of working it out in this life.

Most people in the world are on the spiral path of ascending spirituality, whether they know it or not, and whether they like it or not. Those above you will help you. The ones below you are there for you to help. It is a common chain of friendship that binds men together in the closeness of brotherhood, through which God speaks to us and touches our lives.

How seriously are you committed to living the Golden Rule? Do you or do you not want to do to others as you wish them to do to you? If someone speaks sharply or critically to you, it is frequently an automatic response to reply in kind. This is not the way to learn.

It is easy to forget the little songs of joy that accompany the beginning of each day. Do you recognize the blessings you receive each day, or are you quick to see irritations wherever you turn? Indeed, most snap at families and friends occasionally in spite of their good intentions. Begin to face yourselves with what you do or say. How often have you spoken sharply when your words should have been kind and gentle? Your excuse is "I am tired, or I haven't the patience to be kind today, or I haven't time to think it over." It does not occur to you that these may have been the very thoughts of the friend who spoke sharply to you.

Have you ever asked yourself, "Why am I so willing to see faults in other people"? This is being critical, and in voicing criticism you have no idea how much damage you do with the spoken word. Criticism kills. It kills friendliness, self-esteem, ambition, and stirs up a host of unpleasant emotions. It rasps nerves, and by constant repetition, can cause physical and emotional turmoil. It would be helpful if you could see a balance scale as you utter words. Horror, crime, confusion, worry, criticism, and agitation, are words that have weight because they never rise above the heart. They affect the organs below the heart and the heart itself. Words such as peace, love, mercy, and virtue have no weight so they rise upward drawing your thoughts with them.

The faults of your friends are not your problems or your business. They do not concern you, except that you may be pleased that through the overcoming of their faults, your friends have an opportunity to learn something they need to know. You should see that your friends are intelligent enough to solve their own problems. Do not try to show people what they should do or what to think. Let them think for themselves. This is usually acceptable until your friend treads on your toes, be it ever so lightly! Then you think he should change, but you seldom see that you too, can change.

If you wish to govern your own life so it will be harmonious with other lives, then you should be willing to change when you are wrong. Controlling your mental and verbal reactions to family, friends, and neighbors is a difficult but important task for everyone. How does one live at peace with the behavior of other people resulting from their faults? It is very simple. Realize that very few, if any people in this world are perfect. Then leave your friends free to work out their faults, and you concentrate on correcting your own!

Life is beautiful in its inclusiveness. You should realize that what comes each day are the lessons intended expressly for you. If you are going to fight or resent your lessons then learning them will be much more difficult. If you are disturbed about learning your lessons, you won't get the good out of them. You will remember the disturbance, the uncomfortable feeling, not the lesson. You can prove this to yourself by thinking things over in a quiet, reasonable way. Then they do not seem troublesome. Then it is easier to say, "Well, I'll not let that disturb me again."

You who are sensitive and responsive to hurts should be responsive in the adjustments. A feeling of bitterness toward other people is often most difficult to overcome. Their behavior is meant to be your test, a means by which you learn something about yourself. If you can look at your relationship to others in an impersonal way, their actions can no longer hurt you. What have you learned from certain distressing experiences about your own mental attitude and thinking, that has acted as a magnet for such experiences? Also consider that in certain events, karmic balances may be in process of adjustment in ways that you cannot know in detail.

Instead of being hurt by other people, have compassion for them that they have so much yet to learn. Be thankful that you are coming closer to that place where you can reflect the perfect light of peace and understanding. Be generous and kind in the small ways as well as the larger ones. Great joy may be found by doing a small favor for someone you think has no time for you. Few things bring greater joy to the doer. The surprise also will lift the morale of your one-time enemy. You may even desire to write a nice letter to tell your friend how much you appreciate him. The result will come back so pleasantly to you that you will know that love does work. There are those who can say beautiful prayers. Have they ever thought of writing them down and sending them to someone who is lonely, who may not be able to think of such inspiring thoughts? They make wonderful, uplifting letters. Prayers are often answered in ways we do not understand unless we think deeply about them.

Perhaps God has sent someone to you who needs help. If you do not take what they say to heart, you cannot be hurt, and may be able to let them feel the illumination within yourself. In the 23rd Psalm, those beautiful words, "He leadeth me", speak of the God power to be led. Unless you can accept your lessons and order your lives in accordance with the implications they contain, you will not learn. Seek those things to overcome within yourself, because Christ's victory is a triumphant one over all of life. If you seek to be like Christ, the Overcomer, then act and speak as He taught. In this way you may be free from judging right and wrong, and begin to build your life in the Christ Way of Truth. Let your own life be blessed by letting love and active forgiveness flow forth.

5

OF WHAT USE IS TRUTH?

A search for Truth implies that spiritual knowledge is the goal. For many years, thousands of people the world over have been engaged in an individual search for Truth, and for knowledge of the Divine Laws that underlie all life. These laws do not change as the aeons pass. They want to know personally satisfying answers to questions such as these: Who am I? What is the purpose of life? Is there life after death? Why should I search for Truth? When I find what is true to me, what follows? Is simply knowing Truth enough?

Everyone knows some Truth, but no one has it all, it is much too vast. Living, of itself, provides you with knowledge through experience. Whatever you have found good or true in your life experience, you should keep and go on from there, adding new insights like pearls to a treasured strand. But you should not forget that your emotional reactions to experiences may cause you to reject the spiritual lessons they contain, with the result that the Truths you now think you have acquired so painfully may be distorted and are not true at all.

You need a standard to measure the wisdom acquired by experience. Religion through the ages has offered that standard, and it is a good one, provided there is correct understanding of what is being taught. Now is the entrance of an age when man will turn within himself to find Truth and to find God. You should not be surprised that the God within each man will speak differently. A man is an individual with a particular life pattern to fulfill. When he listens to his Higher Self, he will work out that life pattern without harm to any fellowman. This is the goal of the search for Truth, conscious communion with God, Who waits in unfathomable patience within your own body, knowing one day you will awaken to Him. The sincere desire in saying "Not my will, God, but Thine be done," will lead you to right action and will help you avoid error and pain. Divine laws are few and they are simple. It is man's unawareness or disregard of these laws that has multiplied human problems almost beyond solution.

In seeking Truth, FEEL it is the highest influence in your life, for it helps to lift you to a higher level of living. The desire to know more about God and Truth is a stepping stone to higher knowledge. However there is another indispensable step to be taken which is ACTION. You must find the Truth, make it a familiar part of your mental furnishings, and put it into action in your lives. This is what enables you to make spiritual progress. Most of you have heard people say, "I know much better than I do." What is it within you that prevents you from putting Truth to work in your lives?

There is inertia when you say, "Oh, I'll do it tomorrow." There is reluctance to accept responsibility for lifting your own consciousness. Some people expect to receive from outside themselves. You can receive wonderful things from books, people, and events, but what you DO with these little gems is all important. They must be incorporated into your own being by the power of thought and love for God. Each discovery should make you realize anew His thoughtfulness, compassion, and love in providing everything you, His children, could need for your development into the light. The first thing you need to bring to this upward journey is a self-starter. Your own bodies put up resistance.

They are comfortable in long-established habits and do not want to be disturbed. It is a mistake to let them succeed in resisting what the Spirit desires.

There is failure to understand the importance of ACTION. When you act on what you believe to be Truth, new forces are set into motion in your life. Since you have this high motivation they should be forces for good. This is not always the case however, and you should be prepared for anything when you embark on a course of action. In other words, think an action through to its various possible conclusions, and don't be surprised at unforeseen results. Your neighbors have habits of thought too, and when you do things differently, they will resist the change, or will want to know the reason for it. You should be prepared to tell them in terms that will make sense to them, even if you cannot tell them the whole Truth because they would not understand it.

Keep explanations as simple, logical, and complete as possible. You owe other people this courtesy if the changes you make in your life will affect them, then they will know what to expect of you. This simple act will help avoid much misunderstanding. Also realize, that if the results of your new actions are not exactly pleasant, while you exercise your ability to meet and cope with various situations, you are still receiving invaluable testing. Perhaps you will find that your ability is weak. Very well, strengthen it the best you can, for it is to the strong that the victory is awarded. The victory is not always what you expect. Often it is the victory over self.

If you want your lives to be God-directed, you will find a good part of that direction will come in moments of meditation. Take a few moments for meditation several times a day, especially when a problem confronts you. If you are in the habit of doing this, the answers will come when you need them, without consciously asking, since your Higher Self always knows what you need. Some people never completely lose the sense of oneness with their Higher Self. Whatever else happens to them, their blessings never end. When you have more or less continuous union with your Higher Self, you may ask to learn whatever you desire, and receive direct revelatory knowledge. Think of the value of this in making your lives more productive for good.

Meditation is the laying aside of attention to physical things, and an invitation to your God Mind to impress you with ideas from the fourth dimension. Do not meditate if you are not able to calm your thoughts. Dwelling on disturbing or depressing thoughts will only strengthen them. If you have difficulty getting started, think about a word that will lift your consciousness such as honor, nobility, loyalty, honesty, obedience, tolerance, patience or integrity. All such words have deeper meanings that will be revealed by meditation. Growing in wisdom is an exciting, vital experience through which you may truly feel exalted.

One of the most useful words to think about is EXPECTATION. This quality is outstanding in the good it can bring into being for you. Your thinking mind, directed by your higher God Mind, is very eager to see your entire group of faculties functioning and assisting you in meeting the tests of life. When man can see the existence of the God plan within his physical body and thinking mind, then he realizes how great creation is and will know he is a part of it. However, unless man recognizes something within himself that can be satisfied by the philosophy of any given teaching, the thinking ego will stay right where it has been, possibly for years. Man does not desire change strongly unless there is an urgent NEED. A man must consider what he lacks before he can expect something new to come his way. To be expectant is to make room for something new that will fit or join together with what you already have.

Many people realize the earth is ruled by the power of God. Do you believe God gives to every separate individual a portion of what He considers they are worthy of? No. God does not select those of His choice, letting the hindmost one get what is left. All are served alike and they are privileged to take what pleases them the most. If the seeker on a higher path had not expected to be given a selection of what the spiritual world contains, he never would have endeavored to gain the heights.

So now you have NEED and EXPECTATION. Let us add one more word, OBEDIENCE. Many students start on the path of light but they do not have the patience or endurance to continue. Excuses are many: they do not have the time; they cannot be constantly away from home; or they cannot afford the expense. Obedience to the Higher Self means not permitting these thoughts from your material world to hinder your quest for spiritual Truth.

You must make changes to have results. Almost always you will find change comes about through obedience to the higher direction, aspirations and inspiration. The inspired thought is: "I want to have it. I need it. I desire it more than anything else!" Then the air slowly leaves the balloon when you think, "I can't do that. It would interfere with what I had planned. My family would not like it." Obedience is put aside for the whims and transitory preference of mortal life. The only result is unexpended efforts and unfinished business, because obedience to the Higher Law is put last instead of first.

The Spirit is patient. The Spirit will continue to

inspire your ambition and great desires for your spiritual life, so you may overcome the material things placed in your way. Obedience to Higher Law will bring great reward. But, when you begin to obey, do not question what you will receive as results. Do not allow your thinking mind to ask, "Will it pay? Will its rewards be satisfying?" Obey first, then see the results.

Almost all sermons, regardless of what they refer to, come to the word OBEDIENCE as a basis. Obey the Law of God. You may ask: "What is the Law of God? Which one in that Book am I supposed to obey?" The answer is: any law that is Godly is the same law of obedience. If you obey your Higher Self, then that Law is for you and only you, and you will find many results. For when your happiness is evident, when your efforts are successful, family and friends will look to you as an example to show them the way.

Many people pray for God to do this and that. But we say to you, instead of asking God to do it, do it yourself! There is something Godly in you. When you pray to God, you are praying to your Higher Self, for God is the power of that Higher Self. When you pray for God in you to do something, you become powerful to do it. Again we say, "Obedience to thy Higher Self is spiritual success." Those who believe in prayer must have a sincere expectation of receiving what they ask for. One reason for unanswered prayer is lack of expectation; you turn away from God before He can reply to you.

In referring to the faculty called inspiration, unless the other faculties have also awakened, all information that you receive through inspiration is from one level. (See Chart) When all faculties are open and working, it is like entering a beautiful building with many stories. You are pleased with the first floor, but you want to go higher. Until you go all the way to the top, stopping at every floor, you cannot know its mighty possessions. Each floor is similar to one of your faculties. Imagination is real: it reflects to you things that are real that you do not see. Realization, obedience, aspiration, and comprehension are all mighty qualities that are similar to your intuition, urging you on, enticing you to go one step further. Every time you make an effort of good, there is an urge to do a little more.

Take a long searching look at your habits. Does your Higher Self supervise them, or do they control you? Useless things clutter up your lives and hinder you much more than you realize. Clean out your homes. If you do not actually use an article, why clutter the space in your house? Perhaps someone else can use it.

How do you pray? God knows your needs before you ask; He has given you what He knows is best for you. Let your habits be cleansed and abide in expectation that the highest spiritual Truths will come to you as fulfillment of your particular life pattern.

You may find your own answers to the questions raised at the beginning of this chapter. This is how we have answered them: Each of you is a Divine Being, now and forever. The purpose of life is to unfold that Divinity and to bring as much of it into the light of day as you are capable of expressing.

What is death but spirit ceasing to express itself in the physical world and starting to express anew in another one of the "many mansions" of the Heavenly Father? The goal of the search for Truth is conscious communion with God. Truth needs action to make it the way of self-knowledge and God knowledge.

6

AS A MAN THINKS SO IS HE

The following six chapters are given by Yessue Ben Miriam who walked the earth and was known as Jesus Christ. Yessue Ben Miriam was His given Hebrew name. He does not work from just one Temple on the earth, but He works from all the Temples for the benefit of mankind.

"I give to you the greetings from the Great White Brotherhood. My Soul greets thee. My heart is filled with Love for all fellowmen. I shall speak words of Truth, giving Praise to God on High. Amen. Amen. Amen."

May the peace of the Great Ones that you call Masters or Elohim descend upon each one of you. I, Yessue Ben Miriam, stand in your presence although you do not see Me. I use the voice but not the body of this instrument. The voice is the inner voice that only lives and functions in your Higher Self. As it is often repeated, the voice that you have is a gift. It is the gift of your Higher Self so that you may express.

By hearing the sound you may be able to know and judge what you like or dislike, what is good or not good, so that it reflects on what is commonly called your conscience. Sound affects your conscience until you become sensitive enough to realize that your very thinking is the expression of sounds. If Thoughts are things, everything has its own sound, as well as its own motions and vibrations. You are subject to all sounds and vibrations of motion from anything that exists in your dense world of ether.

I have not come to speak of death. I have not come to go over again that I, Jesus the Christ, was crucified upon a cross. It is enough to say that the body you are living in is a cross. If you stand up and put your arms out you will measure exactly the measurements of a cross, which is the true cross. No matter what direction you face, you still have north, south, east, and west, the directions from which all things come to this earth.

If you could look inside a closed box you would find included in that box, even if it was air-tight, enough atoms to build many lives. If the atoms could be released and used before your eyes, although you eliminate the ether you breath, there is still enough ether in the box to build a universe. No matter how small the box may be, it can contain a universe. A universe means everything that exists upon this earth and in this space around the earth. What you call your universe can be contained in one small container that you could handle with your hands.

So then, how can you see a world around you with your eyes which only see the manifestations of shapes and solid conditions of masses? How can you expect to see the atom that measures so small in your world of manifestation? How can you expect to see and understand it unless you can raise your thinking to Thoughts of the higher realms? These realms are called the dimensions found upon your earth, around your earth, and around each of you.

When you think, you can find the root cause or the Thought that created it. Thought is responsive; you can think about it and be active about it. Now this does not mean that every time you think of something evil, there is an evil Thought, for that is not true. There are no evil Thoughts. The evil is in man's thinking, for he is allowed to make evil from what he thinks about a Thought. If a man desires to destroy another person, the pure Thought is not destruction, the Thought is life. It is the mixture of his thinking that destroys the pure Thought of life until his actions respond to it.

If you feel hatred, it is not because there is a Thought of hate, for there are only Thoughts of love. If you speak of God as the creator, God never contained in any one of His Thoughts of Creation anything that is evil or destructive. It is man's thinking that is destructive. When man's thinking is destructive, he is influenced by some contradiction of natural laws which only exist in your third dimension. In nature, these laws influence the closeness of anything you call nature, and that closeness produces an influence on your thinking. Just as colors can be changed by mixing, so can Thought Patterns become changed by your thinking. This is how your thinking produces the action of illness that you are constantly faced with on earth today.

In the ancient scriptures you will find only the diseases were recorded. Today, it is not as much the diseases but the many illnesses that are brought about because of the thinking of many in your world of action. If a man says there is to be a certain condition of illness such as your cold, the word is spread, and man's thinking produces it. There are many great healers on earth today who teach you to change your thinking so that you will overcome all of your illnesses.

All that is wrong on the earth today is caused by man's thinking. Hate, vengeance, lust, and greed face you whichever way you turn. Those of you who complain that you must pay man's price are standing in your own light. There is an abundance of everything in God's

Kingdom to meet your needs on earth. If man would realize this, he could destroy the markets of lust and greed called competition. Those who are holding the hungry in the palm of their hand and control the food shortages, would be destroyed by their own force.

So you find Thoughts are things and your thinking is a force. Can you not change your thinking? Do not place the responsibility on God's shoulders but on your own shoulders. Your scriptures tell you that every man must bear his yoke. Can you not see that to make a lighter yoke your thinking must change? Can you realize that you can share your thinking of better conditions and prospects so other people may look forward to them?

If you would put forth your own life's effort, the whole world of people could change. It is not accomplished by the sacrifice of death as you can see by the story of My life. It has not only been in the last 2000 years, but in many other opportunities of advancement for man that I gave My life. Yet, all I could give to change man was to show him how to think, and to rise above the conditions that he makes for himself on earth.

When you pass into your shadow body, your invisible or death body, then you can see the difference. You can recognize how you would not do again the things you did on earth, nor would you think the way you did when you were on earth. If you had made changes in your thinking then your whole life pattern would have ended differently, as it should have. When you come back into a physical body again, the memory of that previous life is closed to you in most all ways. You close your own memory until you become conscious that you have lived before. You are here to work out whatever lesson is placed before you, whether it is hate, lust, passion, jealousy or greed. These lessons are here for you to face, and only you can make the changes.

How do you go about making a change? By being

able to think a Truth. If you are jealous, face it. See how you can think differently about jealousy. If it is greed, see what your greed consists of, and how you can think differently about it. If you are greedy of appetite, then you do not trust the God who gave you life. If you are greedy of possessions, then you do not trust that God has given to you abundantly. If you doubt your God, your Higher Self, then you must accept the lesson that comes to you, until there is an acknowledgment in your own understanding of your Higher Self.

For man on earth today, the problems are not the same as they were 2000 years ago or in other times. Your problems bring into the third dimension, those things which you have denied of the higher dimension. These things of the higher dimension could not be given to man on earth before, except in the ages that were destroyed, which you may have heard and known about. God has never stopped in His perfection. The God which gave life, has never stopped molding more perfectly the God Mind in man, and his body that exists on earth, which is a temple of his God Mind.

In the ancient past they did not know diseases that you know and recognize today in your lives. Why? Because the diseases that they knew were of uncleanliness. They did not know how to keep clean. You have had the opportunity to be trained to be clean, and cleanliness is a form of Godliness. If you keep your body clean, your thinking mind clean, and your food clean, you are exempt from many things that people could not have escaped in the past. Many of you believe that you keep your physical bodies clean on the outside, but you do not keep your mental bodies clean on the inside.

Down through the days that have passed since I was Yessue, or Jesus as you call me now, you have had these words preached to you over and over, "Judge not lest ye be judged. Forgive if you desire to be forgiven. Show mercy to those that know not mercy." Yet, how many of you who live on your earth today, let words pass your lips that sound beautiful when they fall upon the ears, but cause harm due to your different mental expressions of thinking. Man is told that it is better to speak the Truth, even though it hurts, than to say one thing and think another.

There are many who profess to be Christians, as your church religions call it, but in their thinking minds they are not Christians. They are pretending. See to it that as you are thinking the Truth, you have no pretense. Even though you speak words that apparently hurt, if it is the Truth as far as you know it is true, be not afraid to speak it. Truth can never harm a Soul. It may hurt vanity, it may hurt personality, but it cannot hurt the Soul of anyone. Do not be so sure of yourself that there cannot be some adjustment to the Truth you believe you have. Be ready at all times to adjust yourself so that you may walk in the light and may receive the light which is Truth.

Light waves surround all Thought. These light waves are not the same as the light on earth you know as daylight or sun reflection but are the light waves of perfection. If a Thought is expressed in imperfection, through imperfect thinking, the light that comes from it is destroyed. In it's place is made dirt, muck, and foreign matters which takes life on earth, wherever they can find room to grow.

There was a time in your history, since I was on earth, when there was a pest of flies. Along with the pests of flies, caused by man's evil thinking, came one of the most drastic plagues on earth. Man creates all that can destroy or cause diseases, by his own evil attractions. With his thinking action, he attracts the destructive things upon the earth. Man then endeavors to find the ways to counteract these pests with poison and destroy them. If he could see what he is actually doing, he would be appalled to find that his own thinking was causing the problem.

I have come at this time of the New Age to be able to help man develop healthy thinking. If he has healthy thinking, he will have a healthy body. How can he have healthy thinking if he does the things that destroy parts of his body that he has no control over?

God has given to each one on earth, whether they are a human being or a mortal being, a universe all their own. You call it the aura; I call it your universe. The outer division of your aura protects your Spiritual Being which you have no control over, except to use it. The center division of the aura makes it possible for the rates of vibration and the waves of sound to pass through your God Mind so that you have contact with the Thought Realm. The inner division of your aura protects your physical body that contains the thinking mechanism so that you are able to image the Thought. You are then able to hold it, name it, classify it and recreate its image, if you so desire.

Within your body you have seven nerve centers, sometimes called chakras, that are protected by sheaths. If you destroy the sheaths that are around your nerve centers, through destructive thinking and habits, then you are destroying your universe. When that is destroyed, it may take thousands of years in spiritland before you can recreate enough of the higher elements to make your universe again. It may take many hundreds of years before you are able to return to earth, because you cannot have the perfection you once had. (See Chart)

All this faces you as you begin to recognize there is something beyond this physical life. Some of you desire to know before you go onto the other side, what your possibilities are, and the exact position you will be found in or placed in. Each of you, if you so desire within your heart, the Great Center of God in you, can know what your future is. Today is the day that you make your adjustments so that tomorrow may reveal to you all that is true of your life, not of someone else's life.

It is most essential for you to be sure that each of you lend a hand to one another. Never let little physical things of personality interfere with that great Christ Love. I do not speak of myself, I speak of the Christ, the Perfection of Love, that is or should be in your lives. If you on earth would cease worrying what other people are doing and live the Christness of yourselves, others would seek to live like you. That is how you help man on earth. Amen. Amen. Amen.

7

TEMPERATURE OF THINKING

"I am Yessue Ben Miriam. I give to you the greetings of the Great White Brotherhood. My Soul greets thee. My heart is filled with Love for all fellowmen. I shall speak words of Truth, giving praise to God on High. Amen. Amen. Amen."

Your earth is the center of the space around it. That space is in the universe around it, and the deep is around this universe. Your mental mind does not extend out into this place of space and deep, and you can only see what you have upon the earth. As you grow not only in years, but in the use of your God Mind faculties, you learn that there is a higher portion of you that can understand what is invisible in manifestation upon your earth. You eventually come to accept that there is something invisible in the higher spaces that affects not only the earth but your bodies also. Here at last, you admit the thinking ability of your mental mind is affected, from without as well as from within.

If the earth has space around it known as the earth aura, and it cannot get out of this aura unless it destroys itself, so likewise, man is in the center of his aura. He cannot get out of it without leaving his physical body. You can understand that the physical man absorbs all he thinks about in some method from his own aura and that he does not think or reason as his neighbor does. Very seldom do we find two or three people that have the same kind of thinking mind or reasoning ability.

Now there must be some division in the aura where a man procures his medium of thinking. His thinking changes not only his way and method of living, but produces the result that he eventually concludes is good or evil; good being that which is constructive; and evil being that which is destructive. Therefore man accepts what produces a good result is due to his improvement of intelligence, and the evil result he blames upon everything else but himself.

Thoughts are things. Those things that belong to your pattern and desires of attraction are in the outer space of your aura. The Thoughts of the development, advancement, or the evolution of your earth, nations, or people are in the aura of space about the earth in the same way. If you understand the multiplication of the magnetism of attraction by millions of minds, you can see how you draw Thoughts deeper into the aura, closer to the earth, within the reach of the mind of man.

Eventually the individual mind of man realizes that he has all the magnitude of power to draw Thoughts or things into his aura that belong to his pattern. He draws first to his human life and its body; second, to his spiritual advancement; third, to his Soul evolution. Man, in his flesh body and thinking mind can draw into his reach from the second division of his aura, beyond the physical level of attraction. He can take apart and image all of the Thoughts and choose his own desires. Therefore, man finds by choosing bitterness, for instance, that it holds the seed of death which you call disease. Bitterness has a great attraction as far as colors are concerned, for it hides all of its defects and only shows the attraction that is pleasing to the eye.

Once man accepts in his thinking mental mind that

death is a problem to solve and overcome, he does not accept that his time is limited. Then he begins to expand out and fight off that which he calls disease and death. Many times it is too late in life because it has gone beyond the balance stage of return. Though he has not overcome death, he has made progress, the step towards overcoming death. Until each individual fights off the cause of death, he must accept the effect. Regardless of how useless a life has seemed and how desperate the death has approached, there has been great advancement.

The results of sin or evil thinking have been classified on your earth in words that carry direct meaning. For example, if you live in hate, you will have what hate produces. If you live in lust and passion, you will disintegrate your body and your mind as well, resulting in incapacity of mind action. If you become a miser, a hoarder, or selfish, you will wonder why nature produces growths in your body, on your body, and in the cavity that holds your brain. You will find that all types of thinking, and the use of the thinking, produce different forms of diseases.

Thoughts are created perfect in their beginning and never leave that place of perfection. Man is the cause of changing Thought by his thinking, by not seeing the beauty of the image of the Thought which is perfect. Then the only healing that can take place is in the thinking world, by the correct imaging of Thoughts that are perfect in the beginning. Mind over matter means the application of thinking in perfection. As you speak, say what your mind and heart within you feels, do not just repeat what someone else has said. It is what emanates from your own thinking mind and the heart center within you, and the force behind it that counts.

As you know, there is a misunderstanding about what is spiritual, what belongs to the higher bodies, and what belongs to the vibrations or the work of your physical bodies. In the physical body you may notice that as you come into the presence of heat or different temperatures, you recognize whether it is hot, warm, mild, or cold. To recognize such conditions, your conscious mind ruling your body must pass through stages to become aware of what is comfortable. Then you realize that the body and body temperatures are changing every hour of your day.

So likewise, there is temperature connected to the thinking ability that rules your thinking mind. When things do not appear true and right, and your conscious awareness is in conflict of how to approach it for better understanding, you call it doubt. But doubt is a temperature. When you say you are fearful of things, it is because you have a sensation you recognize as being scared, but it is a temperature. Now when you feel cold, you have activity only to the rates of your temperature. When you are at a freezing point there is no action whatsoever. The higher your temperature rises in your use of common judgment, the more activity you have. Now we are not speaking of the temperatures that you use in your body as the result of the internal fire consumption you call fevers. We are speaking of the activity of your mental mind, and what your body responds to.

When a temperature is drawn to a body through lust or passion, only the lower extremities of the body or the trunk becomes affected. All organs in the trunk and all ductless glands in the body of the trunk, become creatively affected according to the thinking ability that produces the temperature. This is what causes the creation of results.

When a man is spiritual in his effort of thinking, he does not get below the seat of his brain. He may not be in his higher God Mind activity, he may still be in his physical mental thinking mind. When he becomes truly aware of the nature of all that is around him, he will eventually turn to the nature of his own body. By seeing the image behind all activity, he manifests the temperature of the seeker, and by this activity, creates that particular temperature. This temperature will calm the physical body, but stimulate the intellectual, mental activity. These people are the ones known as students, or the seekers of light.

We find among the seekers of light those that are mild, those that are a little more active, those that are very active, and those that overdo. This is called the temperature of mental thinking. The students who are not able to consume, reason, or understand Truth are always dependent on someone else to tell them what to do and how to do it. They will say they are willing, but they do not search. They expect all of this great intellectual understanding of the Higher Self to be given to them so they can pick out what they want without exerting themselves, and still call themselves spiritual students. We find they are the ones who find fault with how somebody else expresses, or they will say unkind things, because of their sanctimonious attitude.

This type of student will find that he has developed places in his body that are inactive and also places that have become overheated. The result is that the inactive part of his body cannot be used properly, and those parts of his body he considers very active leave deposits that interfere with the natural activities of the body.

I will name a few for you. Some people are always living in fear that their business is going to fail, or they are not able to cope with the efforts of others. They believe that nothing can get along without their strenuous thinking. These people find that they have created acid sores, called ulcers, in their digestive system, caused by the incorrect temperatures of their thinking. Those who are unable to eat normally and while they are eating tear down everything that is honest, will find indigestion is eating away the stomach. It acts on the lining of the stomach caused by critical temperatures upon the saliva that go into the stomach to digest their food and it turns to acid. This is the result of the temperature of their thinking and words expressing their thoughts.

There are those who are envious and always believe that God has given everybody else better opportunities. They believe everybody has acquired what they possess through an error, a sinful stealing, or hiding what does not belong to them. These people will have ulcers through their lower bowels, which is still in the digestive system. The thoughts of the lower world are digested through the lower bowel system. Your medical profession is beginning to recognize this is taking place.

Hate, fear, criticism, and disobedience to normal laws of life or the function of your physical body, place within the heart the actual account of temperatures. For everything that is invisible, a likeness takes place. If you hate, you cannot hate without thinking. You produce a boiling point of temperature that will evaporate or remove all of the good qualities that should belong in your life. As a consequence, you will have aches and pains because you keep these ill-gotten temperatures and their results in your body. You force your heart and lungs to push all this through your circulatory system.

Whenever a wrong thought has been formed, you find that as you think, so it is. The wrong thought goes out from your heart to move through the circulatory system. It deposits what is commonly called rust which is a deposit that will grow and block. The results flow through the bloodstream depositing this rust among the joints, and you call it rheumatism. We teach you that calmness will remove all such deposits. Calmness and any similar activity cause the flow of fluids through the body to be at the right solution to flow easily. The right temperature clears any deposits.

Next we find those who begrudge others. This is not quite the same as enmity. When you have a greedy grudge, it does not always apply to your money. We find those who begrudge any good that comes to another. They begrudge such things as friendship, understanding of Truths, fostering of children, security of home, respect that is in the home and all such activities. When they begrudge those things in the life of others, they build up growths within the circulatory system that are deposited between layers of flesh, or deposits that attack and block what is known as your ductless glands. Then they form tumors, goiters, cysts, and even cancerous growths.

I give to you the ruling laws of nature that belong to the mortal physical body, the steps called the gates of death. It all depends on temperature. You go to the extremes of chills or to the extremes of fevers: it is all temperature. When you mingle both of them together, the inactivity of your intelligence allows ignorance to form germ life, by temperature. You overcook your good thoughts, or you overcook your evil thoughts by temperature, and the result is death. You are decomposing or dismantling by disease, the house that God gave you to live in.

Every disease comes under either chills or fevers, excitement or hate. Regardless of the many types, they are classified as indigestion. You cannot have a digestive system actually working as God intended while you mingle your thinking with hate, anger, lust, passion, greed, or enmity. It all leads to the destruction of your connection to the God Self. Then you have rust in its many forms of aches and pains. It goes through the circulatory system and your respiratory system, and the lymph glands create a solid substance, instead of a fluid substance. It may create a matter form that is called humor with germ. Then you classify it as asthma, bronchial, tuberculosis, sinus, catarrh and many other diseases.

Some have secrecy in their actions, trying to live a pretense of the spiritual life so the world may see how good they are. If you are hiding all the evil intentions, your results will be the tubercular, lung, or respiratory conditions. Secrecy of passions and avarice in thinking produces germ life.

I am Yessue Ben Miriam, and I have given you these things to think over to help you understand your own creation. Amen. Amen. Amen.

8

WASTED EFFORT

"My Soul greets thee. My heart is filled with Love for all fellowmen. I shall speak words of Truth, giving Praise to God on High. Amen. Amen. Amen."

I am the man named Jesus who walked the earth. I am a Son of God. Beloved children of earth, you also are Sons of God. If it was possible to give you the true meaning of all I spoke, there would be clearer manifestations of Truth. Those who knew the language of the ancient time, did understand the meaning of the words I spoke. However, like many of the people in all nations and tribes upon the earth, whatever is the easiest and most pleasant to manifest is what man accepts.

Most often, those in your group of acquaintances who have more in possessions or education, are the ones who are looked up to as authorities. An authority does not always know Truth, and sometimes it is partly true and partly false. So the layman, even though he seeks a better understanding, is often misled because his effort is not aimed for the higher or inner interpretation of Truth. The good and the bad, as you classify them, are those who are learning by the destructive expression or the constructive impression. Can you be sure which side you belong on?

Those of you who complain daily about your trials

and tribulations, or disturbance of inharmony and confused thinking about them, are wasting your better energies and opportunities by ignorant speech. I would call it a wasted effort. Those who are having their test of how much faith they have, whether they need to have more faith, or know where to turn to find that faith, will never find it by wasted words. They need to know how to turn within, and contact that great energy that is constantly flowing from the heaven to the earth, which is called God's Blessings.

Those who are ill are constantly making mistakes, errors or sins, that mar the generation of energies in their bodies. It mars the generating activity and motivation of the body. Until they suffer, they do not know that they are mixing, confusing, and destroying their good qualities. Therefore, their sickness, aches, or pains are only in the thinking mind.

Now we do not tell you that the pain is not real, or that the cause is not real that makes the pain. We simply say, their erroneous thinking and inability to think clearly is causing the pain and discomfort of their body. Unless they seek to know how to change their thinking, it is constantly with them, to disturb, agitate and cause them to seek a higher elevation of thinking. Those are what we term the discomforts of your physical body. We do not classify them as the sins of the seven deaths.

The sins of the seven deaths are the diseases that destroy the physical body in its perfection. As these sins destroy the physical body in perfection, they also destroy part of the God Mind in man. When you separate the God Mind from man by any part of the physical organs, ductless glands, faculties, or the centers, you are separating man from God. It destroys the motivation of God's power of living life, the Spirit. There is nothing on earth, or in the earth power that can change it, unless the man is filled with the desire for God's perfection.

When you can teach anyone who has a clear thinking mind, teach what faith is; what hope is; what peace is; what love is; and what harmony expresses. Until you can inspire them to desire these things, God cannot work in them. He can work on the outside of them, but not within them. On the outside of their aura, in the spiritual division, God is ever working. When it comes to the separation between the Spirit and the mortal man being, only man can reconnect the separation. Death in most cases of separation is the result, because man will not change. Man must change his understanding and comprehension, and have willingness to accept the Spirit instead of repel it. He must give up his mortal attempt and accept that which is immortal.

Now I have spoken in words, and as I demonstrate in your thought picture form, I would like you to use them together for a greater understanding. In your physical division of the aura, all of the elements that belong to your particular body are reproduced every twenty-four hours. If you do not use them, they become wasted as far as your physical body is concerned. Then the earth sucks or draws them in. The field of magnetism is so great on and in the earth, that the little bits of energy that belong to one human being are like a needle in a haystack.

In the second division of the aura, called the Soul division, the changes take place from the great power of the elements that descend to the Soul pattern of a Son of God. That Soul pattern never changes. The Soul in this division must change the spiritual energy to adapt to your human mind.

Let us look at the evolution called incarnation and reincarnation. The Son of God is only one life but your physical body may have many, many lives. What percentage of this body that you are living in now, is in the reception of its spiritual quality? If all the other bodies had used some up, how much spiritual quality do you have left? That is a picture that I would desire each of you to understand. Each time you come on earth, you have a percentage of what is left of your Divine Self to work with. Not until you have evaluated all the energies that you have lost, misused, or even imposed upon others, can you be joined in perfection to the Son of God, Elohim.

The first destruction that the Soul must watch, is the destruction of the pattern of life. This is called the step of death. Whatever pattern holds the lessons that will teach man his Soul is supreme over the perfection of the physical body, is how man learns not to misuse any of the energies that come from the higher space for his particular use. So Divine Healing, as you term the perfected law, is achieved with the understanding of the Soul, not the mental body. The Soul controls man's efforts, ambitions, higher impulses of inspiration, his longings, hunger and thirst for greater things. In each stage of death man learns about the power of God, either while he is in his physical body, or when he has passed through the change of death.

The seven steps of death are chosen by man for his own pattern when he comes to earth. The ills of the body, known as mental sicknesses or disturbances, are not set diseases, though they can open the door wide for disease to take place. How does man set the law of disease that is called the law of death? Man sets the law by knowingly going against Truth and submitting to habit. To submit to any habit that destroys the nerves, the nerve senses or the nerve centers that function in the centers of sense and thought, sets the laws of death.

Though you may be wrapped in death, and the

breath of life has left the body, as long as the mind has control, it can return if your pattern is not finished. The man who would work as I have worked for my Father, must forget self, and must close his eyes to what is before him. His spiritual eye will show him exactly what is wrong, as to the Soul being forced to watch the habits man on earth so easily follows.

Let us look at some habits. Man will let his appetite cause a disease through the digestive system. He will misuse that system by overeating, under-eating, and crudely eating. He will indulge in the habits of pleasure or the disbursement of the Divine energy that is often called pleasure. This is a desire of possession. When you desire to possess something, it crowds out the God in you.

Habit claims those who are never still long enough to allow the God in them to work, or who are too busy in worldly affairs, or too physically tired to commune with the Higher Self. Acceptance of things that numb and destroy the nervous system, such as habits of intoxication, smoking, the use of nicotine in any form, or the use of drugs, destroys the activities of Truth, and destroys God's movement in man. These things destroy the nervous system, and are what disconnect the spiritual man from mortal man. The Soul cannot put anything into a body if it cannot find a place to put it.

We find a man who has anger and hate, repulses all the perfected energies that flow into his blood stream. Hate and anger thickens the blood into clots until it forms tumors and cancerous growths. We find those who are envious, vain, or lust after power, close the energy that is in the air they breathe, and set the law of death.

When I worked on the earth, I did not see what manifested on the outside; I saw what was manifested in a person's aura. The only way a divine healing can take place is when man's inner eye can be opened long enough to let him see how to connect his higher power with his lower power. This is the connecting action of the natural law and the nature law. Nothing is impossible when the natural law can take action over and consume the nature law.

I shall explain if you will permit your mind's eye to go to a high space and mingle among the celestial stars, far above the planets. There, power is created and descends to earth. It is not one power, but twelve different kinds of power descending toward the earth. Each one of those powers has a work to perform on earth, called the movements of God. Each one has the ability to create twelve kinds of elements called principles in your Bible.

Those 144 different kinds of elements create the chemicals that belong to earth and to mortal man's body. Of these, there are twelve elements that constitute the essence of Spirit, Prana and Mind. If it takes twelve of those hundred forty four elements to perform each separate part of essence, prana, and mind, you have thirty-six elements that constitute your Spirit, Soul and Mortal bodies.

In your mental mind, you may see the elements descending to earth as a ray or sunbeam. Yet, they are filled with patterns; the molecules of energy as atoms of a pattern. That which descends down into the dense ether around earth is what you receive in your nature laws and as your pattern of mental thinking. That which descends through the creation of your light ether is received by Spirit and God Mind.

If you could see the molecules, as they descend into the dense ether, you would see little balls of light that burst open and let millions of atoms loose in the dense ether. Here each atom becomes a living, moving thing. It takes shape according to the law it belongs to in the kingdoms on earth. Those elements or atoms that belong to the human kingdom, never descend into anything else. What belongs in the animal kingdom does not descend into any other pattern. According to its kind, so it is. When the deposits of elements reach the earth, they are as pure as any part of the divine elements created from the powers of God. When the deposit of your Soul accepts your pattern, they are shining particles of gold. However when they get in touch with the physical laws of earth, they become tarnished and covered, and there is no light. This change takes place through your thinking.

Seek to find yourself worthy, for daily you are walking in the Light of God. In your true nature, you are the Son of God. Everything that God brings to you is exactly what He has asked you to meet. Every unkind word comes to make you think so that you may see the difference between kindness and unkindness. The purpose of every struggle you feel you lack understanding to overcome, is to turn you to your Higher Self that knoweth all things. Nothing is impossible with God.

When something is given you to do; God is asking you to do it. Do it, not only for Him, but for your Higher Self. If this is accomplished, you will see the healing manifestations of the Spirit, which is more important than the healing of the body. Man has but one Spirit, but he has many bodies. There is not one body that will ever sit on the throne by God, only one Spirit. Amen. Amen. Amen.

9

CHANGE YOUR WAYS

"I am Yessue Ben Miriam. I am known as Jesus Christ, who walked your earth and gave to man in this age, the Light of Salvation. My Soul greets thee. My heart is filled with Love for all my fellowmen. I shall speak words of Truth, giving praise to God on High. Amen. Amen. Amen."

I shall speak so that you may understand that I, Jesus Christ, walked and healed on the earth. I shall not go back farther than two thousand years ago when the preparation was made for me to be born in a flesh body on earth. This occurred so man could find the Higher Self, within himself, and become as Jesus the Christ, as well as I, who came and walked among them.

Now if you will correctly understand the meaning of the mother Mary, the father Joseph and Myself, we did not come through spiritland and this is called the virgin birth. In reality, I was not born of a virgin, as you know it. A virgin means one who descended to the earth from the higher realms to prepare the way, so I could take on physical life and be in a position to teach the people who walked the earth at that time.

If you will allow your intelligence to go back 2000 years, you may see the difference between the people who walked the earth then and those on earth now. At that time, people did not know about the many things that you know today. They did not see the things that you see in your physical world, manifested in the objects of your daily living. Their lives were free and in the open much of the time. You will also remember very few earth disturbances were spoken of, except lightning, thunder, and earthquakes. After the great flood, very few things happened that disturbed the physical man in his daily living.

Their constant walking and eating natural foods built a strong body. Man on earth today does not know about the type of body that existed two thousand years ago. Today, man seldom walks upon the earth, but he has much between his feet and the earth. Today the food is so changed that man is eating himself to death. Now, when I say to death, I mean destroying the physical body. First, he does it by his fearful thinking. Second, he does it by not eating normally. Today, man's body is not the same type of body that they had many years ago.

Today, you do not have the contacts with contagious diseases that were so prevalent in those days. Man of 2000 years ago did not know how to live without the contamination of impurities, or know how to care for food the way you do today, yet the systems are the same. Your physical body is built around an energy field of attraction. However, man does not pay enough attention to realize, that as he thinks, so he attracts. Whatever you have in your field of attraction, you have in your system called your solar plexus.

This magnetic field attracts out of the ether, from the air around you, and from contacts with people. This field of magnetic force attracts thinking, as well as Thoughts or Ideas. It is the field of attraction for Ideas, Thought and thinking. When your thinking penetrates into another person's field and they desire to make a similar attraction, they attract what you are thinking.

Then it reflects into their consciousness so that they can be attracted or repelled by you, or you are attracted or repelled by them. No man has the right to interfere with any other man's thinking.

You have within your own mind a great looking-glass called your imagination. Some of you only use it to see the little things upon earth that someone else has created, without any of your effort, except that you place a value on it. If you only use your imagination this way, you'll never know the sweetness of its creation. This mirror within each one of you, called a solar plexus, is a magnetic force. It draws out from the ether what you are not able to see until it comes into manifestation.

There are seven levels of this magnetic force. First, you draw or attract what you need so your body can grow physically. The first level of attraction contacts the energies to build and sustain your body. They attract to you the exact pattern from the ether that belongs to you and no one else. As long as your body is not interfered with it will be a Natural Law for you, and will be over the nature laws. The moment a body has been interfered with, you must have help to obtain enough energy to sustain it. This is called a healing.

If you will notice the records of healing, when I healed the man and said, "Go and sin no more," the interpretation is not exactly as I had stated. If you had heard it, you would know I said, "It is your thinking of fear, doubt, and lack of faith, due to lack of understanding, that causes you to sin and create the disease you have been healed of. Learn to think, and as you think, all things take their rightful place within your system. Then you will not have disease and sickness."

It is said that Saul became Paul overnight, but that is not true. He spent a great amount of time in the invisible fourth dimension before he realized the life he spent on earth as Saul was wasted. When he came back as Paul, he lived in the Light, taught in the Light, and proved his Higher Self was always present, even in the mire. It is by the pitfalls as well as the successes that man receives the Truth for himself.

One of the questions often asked is, "How can I, Yessue Ben Miriam, appear everywhere and still be One?" There is no limitation of time, distance or space in the fourth dimension. Though I come from a higher dimension, I work on earth in the fourth dimension. In this Christ body, there is representation with no limit to its number, which can be called everywhere. There will be no separation with you, when you are able to control your thinking mind so that pure Thoughts flow freely in you. Your Higher Self will be in every Thought that goes out from you.

Now I would desire to tell you of the polarization that comes from the earth that is called the odic force. This odic force enters from the earth into your body through your feet, regardless of how you stand, sit, or lie. Do I hear someone say, "Suppose they do not have feet?" In your visible world maybe they do not have feet, but in the world that is invisible to you, the feet are normal. The vibrations enter in the lowest point at the heel of your foot. This earth vibration holds you to the earth and keeps you as a normal human being upon the earth.

At the same time there is a golden cord above your head, like a halo would be, whether you face north, south, east, or west. This cord extends out into space even beyond the fourth dimension. Through it must come all the directness of spiritual force and energies that enter into your body. These invigorate your brain cells and all of the nerve centers in your body, and maintains your living pattern or seed. When you pass out of this body, that seed never dies. Your seed is made to the pattern you were born on earth with, and resides in the invisible side of life with your invisible self, called your shadow self. Until you are able to take on another physical body form, the seed is idle. It is useless on the invisible side until you are born again in earth life.

Now what do you bring back with you when you return to earth? You bring back all the mistakes, the misfit ideas, and the problems you could not solve before. You bring the harm and injuries you have caused others. You bring what you lack most; respect for yourself. Lack of respect for yourself means you have not stood upon your own feet as a Son of God.

These are the problems you bring back to earth. You do not bring any golden crown back with you or any of the good deeds that you happened to have made or completed upon this earth. When you come back to earth all these problems face you daily. Sometimes, at an early age, you have overcome those problems that relate to your youth. As you grow older, it becomes clear to you what you failed in before, and are you moving towards failure again?

How do you know and recognize these things? I shall tell you. There are seven conditions or gates of death. They are chills, fever, germs, indigestion, rust, evaporation and decay. These are created by the seven deadly sins: hate, anger, lust, envy, greed, jealousy and passion. These deadly sins cause the disease that will bring death. By the name or type of the disease you will know what you have failed to accomplish. Let no man tell you that the diseases are God's problems or that the diseases are God's way of helping you leave the earth. God never created anything that harms any man. Man alone has created all of these problems.

It is true that God has given His ministering angels charge over you. It does not tell you that some of the angels are the evil angels that make you learn your lessons whether you desire to learn them or not. You call them evil because they do not fear you, nor do they fear to do what is necessary to be done. Therefore, if you have many pains or tortures, it is because they are helping you to find your problems. They do not hide problems away and say, "We do not like to see you suffer." They delight in seeing you suffer, for the more you suffer, the greater the Truth is born within you.

There are those of you on earth whose heart's desire is to do good, and whose aims are always for the best. However, little irritating problems such as too much sympathy for some, or lack of understanding of which way to turn to do the best will stand in the way of a successful healer such as Jesus. If you remember His words, there were places He could not do any healing because of their unbelief. Though I like to tell you instead, there were some cities He could not heal because of their unbelief. The interpretation of the word "cities" means mysteries.

People are so consumed within their existence that they can not be healed because of their unbelief. Some people you come in contact with are so distracted by this, that and the other, that they cannot do anything correctly or perfectly. They have no desire to correct one thing, for fear it would interfere with something else. There is no half way for anyone, it is all or nothing.

When Jesus was passed the cup of death He did not pass it by, although He could have. He knew by His very death many would learn the Truth. If He had saved Himself, they would never have found the Truth. So why do you take it upon yourself to sympathize with those who are having their problems or troubles? If they must have their pain, let them have it. Bless them, for they shall find the Truth. Know that in God's own time they shall learn the Truth, for you cannot unravel the

Truth for them. They do not tell you that it is their conscience that is causing the suffering and the pain. If they asked to be freed from the sin or guilty conscience, they could be free of their aches, pains, and the disturbances in their body.

If you consider the foods that different people eat, and believe this is good and that is bad, then you are dividing God. We do not tell you that you must change your attitudes or your way of living. We simply teach that you can change your thinking to know that there is nothing in God's kingdom, or His creation that can harm you. You cannot be divided that this is not good, and that is good. A divided thought cannot produce action, and that is exactly what many of you on earth are doing. Whatever God sets before you, be thankful, be gracious enough to accept that God has placed it there in its purity for you.

Concerning many of the foods that are on your earth today, we recognize that too many things are being added to them. We realize they are not in their natural form. We say, if those of you who constantly feel that you can get it here or there, in a purer state than you can buy it in another place, you are mistaken. If, for example, impurity is found in the source of the sweetness of your honey; in the nectar of the blossom and if the bee is diseased, it is in the honey. If you eat the honey believing that it is all pure, as long as you can believe, beyond doubt or question, that honey will never bother you. But the moment you say, "I wonder if this honey is free of impurities, I wonder if this honey is better than the others, or if this one is not as good as the others", in the moment that question has entered into your conscious mind, you have a divided attitude of good and bad.

I say it is good if you only have a glass of wine and a slice of bread. If you can have all faith that this is what

God has provided for you, your body will respond to every part of it and nothing can hurt you. When you have a piece of fruit, an apple, a pear, a banana, or any other kind of fruit that you like, if you question for one minute that it has been covered with something that should not be on it, it is going to poison you, regardless of whether it had anything on it or not. If you can believe that nothing on it can hurt you, it cannot hurt you. It is the thinking that produces good or evil, the wrong source or the right source.

What God places before you is what God intends for you to eat. It is the same with your thoughts. Many Thoughts can be placed before you, but because there are several thousand Thoughts placed before you does not mean that you must remember every one. It does not mean that you should immediately start changing your life pattern to live as these words have said. Every Thought expressed in words is for you to think about. What you think is what builds your life as it is. "As a man thinketh in his heart, so is he", it is said. This applies not only here but when he passes to the other side, so is he. The purpose of man suffering from his ills, is to make him think and to change his ways. It is true here on earth, that even if I stand by your side, I cannot heal anyone who will not change his pattern of life.

Now, let us look at the word hate. Those who hate, curdle or burn their own blood. It thickens so that it cannot flow through their veins. The result produces clots or blotches somewhere in their body. In time it will affect not only their brain but other parts of their body, and produce a disease that will cause much disturbance. Hate causes chills and fevers which will work upon the blood also.

Now let us take the word, lust. Thou shalt not lust. Lust and fear produce about the same results. To lust after a thing, means you want something that someone else has, but you fear you are not capable of taking it from them, without them finding out. Fear causes a digestive disturbance. Anger will do the same thing. Anger will not cook the blood, but causes the digestive gastric juices to cease flowing. What flows is like poison. This is how you are creating your own poisoning, because it disturbs the digestive system; nothing will produce good that has been poisoned by anger.

Next, let us speak about those who crave or are greedy. Greed is hoarding. You earn money, perhaps by labor, and hide it away instead of buying or using it for things that are needed for yourself or those around you. You hide it away only to lose it in time. While this greed works in you, you are possessive and greedy of other people's goodness and their good actions. You turn inward with hate and anger, as much as with greed on the outside. This will produce blotches, tumors and so forth through the system, often causing kidney trouble. Sometimes it will hinder the breathing and cause disturbance in the lungs.

Let us return to passion of the body. When man has abnormal passions he uses for self satisfaction rather than creative purposes, it burns up the energy that is intended to rebuild the body. This will cause a decrepit condition. They will find they have deformed bodies in their later years and sometimes even before the later years. Many times, passion produces a deformity or an unnatural condition in sex. This destroys the Soul quality pattern.

For those who turn away, let us look back to the story of Lot and salt. What went wrong there was that sin became evil: man after man, and woman after woman, and it became a lost city. That is what passion is turning this world into today, not only in this country, but in almost every country. Except I will give an honorable, clear chart for the Chinese and the Japanese. In all of the eastern European countries, they are also bringing death upon themselves, and they shall turn into pillars of salt.

Now the meaning of salt is this: salt burns but it purifies. Salt is like gravity because they will be held to the earth. Those that are called evil ones shall work them over. Those who perform unnatural conditions bring about cancer, which is the most dreaded disease upon your earth today. As hate will bring on heart trouble, so you will find the evils of passion bring on cancer. So by the steps of sin you enter through the gates of death.

When a person has avarice in their appetite, they have secrets hidden within themselves. It is abnormal for anyone to be overweight. There is something that they are hiding within themselves. They attempt to use their appetite for food to keep at peace within themselves. The satisfaction of the stomach is sometimes the satisfaction of the conscience. There are those who create certain diseases by eating too much of certain types of food. When they cannot cease eating the foods that harm them, they have become pleased with what they have. They get sympathy, and are looked upon as needing comfort and help. They want pity. Children use this behavior when they are afraid to grow up and be normal.

Let us look to the older people. There are those who have dropsy or too much liquid in their body. When they know that and do nothing about it, they must like it. There are those who drink to excess of that which poisons the system. If they cannot or will not do anything about it by themselves, they must like it. There are those who use the destroyer of their aura, the nicotine in tobacco. Regardless of what kind of tobacco it is, it is harmful.

They destroy their own bodies, only to have to create more bodies over and over again, until they can free themselves of their habit. It is lack of will power not to rise above their five physical senses with a little bit of thinking, reason, or imagination. Man must consider, whether he wants the destruction of habit, or not. It is because they are afraid to think clearly for themselves. No man can say he cannot stop smoking if he is willing to think about it.

You have free will to make choices so you must learn how to use this will in your thinking mind. You will receive the results of your own thinking, until you learn to dissolve the errors, and become the overcomer of self and death. Amen. Amen. Amen.

10

THE WAY OF THE CROSS

"My Soul greets thee. My heart is filled with Love for all fellowmen. I shall speak words of Truth, giving praise to God on high. Amen. Amen. Amen."

Beloved students of the earth, with understanding, the parables can all be interpreted and explained. In the Bible, it speaks of your hands and your feet. Can you imagine a God, a creator of love, who would have you cut your hands or your feet off, crippling you for your life? Can you imagine what was forgiven one, would not be forgiven another? The hands mean power, and you have a right and a left power. You, as man on earth, both visible and invisible, use these powers. They represent the hands of good and evil, in your thinking world and in your Christ consciousness. Your feet, often referred to as clay, represent the vibrations that you find on earth. These vibrations begin with the energies that come from the earth, to physical man.

When the Bible speaks of the world, it does not mean the planet that you are born upon. It means your own world of your own making, your high or low understanding of it, and the generations you have lived in existence to find salvation. Children represent the simple version of Truth that man so often passes by. Most would rather have some outlandish performance or glorified words to reach their God. All you need to do is think in order to reach your Higher Self, called the Me of you, your Soul in action.

In the parables, you find they ask, "Who is the greatest in heaven?" Since there are several heavens, which one are they referring to? First, the heaven on earth is where you adjust or join together the positive and negative manifestation of your flesh body and lower thinking mind, to be harmonious with your higher thinking mind or the Thought World.

Then, we find the man who could not forgive. Seldom on your earth, regardless of the many attempts, have you forgiven your material body or your material world, for leading you through the tests you must pass through on earth. When we say "forgive", we are speaking of your invisible self, called your invisible flesh body. It is constantly with you so you can interpret every intention. It forgives you many times, but you demand of it and your Higher Self, great things that you are not always worthy of.

The first contemplation that each of you should find is the forgiveness of self. It requires an attitude of, "Forgive me Father, for my errors in my earth life. Forgive and show me the light that I may create a new world, a new possibility of freedom." Remember, until you have forgiven your own creation, you have not been able to forgive others. What others do is not your concern. As the individual, you may have asked for the test or trial, and God has answered. So you have no one to forgive but yourself. Then, forgive the ignorance and the interpretations, that are preached to you all over the world.

When you simplify Truth, you take all the glamour away from it. We seldom find those on earth who claim they are seeking the Truth, that will take it in the simplified form. Glamour must come with every word and action. Attractions by the energies of earth must hold you or you lose the highest interpretation and interest.

When My Father in Heaven sent Me to earth, I took on a flesh body as Abraham. As Abraham, I learned the beginning steps of life. Throughout that generation and all through the times I came to earth, the records have proclaimed I was this, that, and the other. Each time, I was simply the Son of God, taking on a flesh body and giving the Truth to the people on earth. All the popular interpretations present glamour and falseness. When it came time to enter the earth as the man Jesus the Christ, I was able to touch on the most important steps. I taught that you must become as little children to learn at the foot of the throne. Little children mean your simple or simplified thoughts, without any glamour or painting of glory.

When I was asked, "How shall I pray?", I gave a very simplified and Truthful prayer of My Father Who art in Heaven. Heaven is the state of consciousness of the awareness of the Higher Self. There is no God above you to listen to all of your glamorous words. The only help that you can receive is to free yourself of man-made ideas, get down to the simple Truth, and give up self impressions that lead you astray. Give up the desire to know the Truth, yet, accepting what is not true. Know ye not that all men are Gods? Born into your environment and life pattern is the pattern of the Elohim, Son of God. You need not beg or implore: you simply ask and it shall be done unto you.

I refer to the words of your Bible that say, "You must be baptized again." Baptism means that you are washed of the untruth, and see light as Truth. Unless you can recognize your own errors, there is no man on earth that can wash them away. No man who ever lived on earth could wash them away, as it all depends on you. I do not mean that you should not share with others your pleasant and beautiful thoughts, but when you pray, simply pray "Our Father Who art in Heaven." When you seek to do good on earth in your physical lives, and speak from spiritual interpretation, you pray to the Father in Heaven. He is in constant contact with your state of conscience, and your states of consciousness, to bring you or draw you closer to the Thought Realm, where all Truth is explained.

You read in the Bible that a multitude of people followed Me along the shore, walking the sands for many miles to hear the word as I gave it from My Father in Heaven. They did not complain of being weary because they had to tarry by the wayside, they were seeking the staff of life. The staff of life is the need of the physical body that you refer to as bread. The maintenance of your spiritual mind, through Thoughts, is represented by fishes all through the Bible. If you look for the symbols, you will find the words that fit.

When we preach that the world is coming to an end, it is quite true. But rest assured, the earth will never come to an end. The Earth is the planet which your creation was adapted to. The World is your environment, capacity of thinking, and ability to reach out and touch the invisible world. This is simple Truth without any glamour, and everyone should be able to accept it. When you read the Bible parables, endeavor to interpret them correctly and ask for help so you may understand.

I have told you about the region of spiritland you may enter when you leave the earth by death. I have also shown how you can be reborn by leaving your invisible body, and taking a new pattern on earth again. I have shown you where the Kingdom of the Great White Brotherhood is located in consciousness. You are incapable, in most cases, to aspire to the heights of the fourth and fifth dimension. When you are obligated to return into spiritland through death, decay, sickness, inharmony, aches and pains, discord and diseases, you lay aside your physical body. When the angels that God has given charge over you see that you are ready to return to earth, you bring back what you have not forgiven to work out.

Do not complain because your trials and tribulations are many. Do not complain when your heart aches with grief, because with your endeavor, you can overcome it all. My Father in Heaven has never permitted you, at any time, to take on a burden or a pattern of life, unless He absolutely knew you were big enough to overcome it. God does not punish; you punish yourself. When you commit error, it is because you have not learned the lesson correctly. When you sin, it is because you do not understand, and that understanding must be earned. When you forgive those who sin on earth, you shall understand why they sin. Then you are able to bring about a reckoning of their consciousness, so they can understand the day of judgment that all men on earth pass through.

You have heard that the councilors of this Temple and other Temples, have certain names. Those names are not the names that were given to them when they were born on earth. The names are given as the reckoning of their forgiveness, by Almighty God. Then they could ascend into the Kingdom that I spoke of as, "In my Father's House are many mansions, and I go to prepare a way".

It plainly states in your records that I gave up My physical life of My own accord. I laid down My physical life so man could see that he had other lives. Those who could not understand needed a demonstration. I reappeared on the third day after death to show that I lived again. Even though I died of flesh, I lived again. So may you as you lay down your physical life. Make your effort now so you do not have to enter into spiritland, but can ascend to that land where you descended from, before you came to earth. That land is the Kingdom of the Masters.

We have chosen to use the name Masters, so it would not be confused with those in spiritland who have earned the ability of freedom to help man on earth. The spiritland helpers are often referred to as guides, directors or teachers with great understanding. There are also those in spiritland who would destroy you, to keep you on earth so they may return and go through their pleasures and sensations.

The Masters of the Third Kingdom have overcome death and all such trivial things of flesh. Their love is holy and their understanding is pure. God has given them charge over the people called the Israel. If you do not understand this, it is possible you have not read the records of your Bible. When you overcome death, you ascend into the second heaven. In the second heaven, you do not take on flesh bodies again, unless you are sent to earth to recreate certain Truths for man's understanding.

In the Kingdom of the Masters, there are seven realms. The first three are called the Great White Brotherhood, interpreted from the word Melchizedek. Melchizedek means: evolution by ascending over death. You evolve in the kingdom of the Masters, the same as you evolve on earth, or ascend from earth.

Let us look at the first plane or area in the Master Kingdom. There you will find those who have selfishly gathered power over beings, and they are in charge of the races on earth. They cannot leave that realm because they are mixing up the races or bloods on earth. The true Israel has pure blood, regardless of his race. He never mixes it with any other race, for if he does, his pattern cannot be true.

In the second realm of the Master Kingdom reside those who work with governments or nations, and there are evil forces as well as the good forces. To destroy one another's nations or governments, is the prime act of the dark forces on earth. These masters may have overcome death, but work with Satan, the Devil, and Lucifer. They would blind man destroying his intelligence with false hopes, false truths, and false abilities.

The third realm of the Great White Brotherhood is the true Melchizedek order. They have obligated themselves to bring through all of the purified blood life on earth, who began with Abraham, through to the Christness or Son of God. They are in charge of all those seeking light on earth. Now light only emanates from understanding, from the seventh center, and your God mind.

When you speak of your heart, seldom do you know what you are talking about, for the heart is the core, the center of your existence. It does not mean the organ in your body. So why do you, waste your time with useless words, to proclaim the glory of God? God is and always has been, but there is only one Almighty God. "Thou shall not proclaim any other God before Me, but Yehovah." The word Yehovah means four Gods of unadulterated power. They have created the Israel race, so the Elohim may come and partake of the greatness of the earth and bring home the reward, the harvest, that you on earth are called.

I never proclaimed while I was on earth that I was the only Son of God. It is a parable. Only the Elohim are the Sons of God. Because it says Son, it does not mean one. It means all who are working on that plane of existence for mortal man, for the human man, and for the being that came on earth long before the Elohim descended to earth, and before the Israel existed on earth. If you will acquaint yourself with your True Self, you will understand my words as Truth.

The prayer that is ever before the Elohim, in the heavenly kingdom is: "That not one of you shall ever want for Truth or ever be led astray."

I will endeavor to answer your questions now. If you raise your vibration, which is the great emotional nature of your higher mind, not your body, I can come as often as needed. I walk and talk with you, yet, you hear me not. You think it takes a physical body for you to hear, but that is not true. If you raise your faith and belief, great enough to reach the heaven, I can walk and talk with you and teach you the story of life.

Q. Master, in sending out the light as I mentioned this morning, I don't think of it being the physical heart center, but the center of great love, and that is what I meant. I didn't really refer to the body.

A. I am quite sure you did not refer to the organ in the body. But I am telling you, that before you is a great sun, where all energy emanates. The energies go to those who open their minds to receive, and their needs to be filled. That is called the great light. It does not come from your sun, it comes from the great light that is called the White Light of the Heavenly Father, who brings it to you from the Kingdom of Almighty God.

Q. Would you tell of the parable of the crucifixion?

A. The parable of the cross was not a tree that I was supposed to struggle up a hill with. I took on a physical body that was My cross, and that is your cross too. What I killed were the great habits, desires and sins of the physical body in man, to show that all must be the overcomer. When it speaks of the man on the cross that each side held, I can explain that, for I crucified myself by taking on the cross. The thief on the left side is interpreted to mean how the great power of physical man can mislead, but the Christness in all men forgives. The man on the right side represents your false illusions, delusions, impressions, and beliefs. As long as you have them you will have war by swords and horrible deaths. Until man is ready to give up his falseness for Truth, there will be leaders. These leaders must take up their cross and bear the earth existence to help find freedom for others.

Q. Can you tell us again that the cross we take up is never more than we can bear.

A. That is a promise My Father has given from His Heaven. He first sees you capable of bearing every burden or cross that is needed. He sees you are great enough, before He permits you to take up your cross. When you are on the other side, in your invisible physical body, preparing to return to earth, your Guardian Angel is quite capable of adjusting the pattern that you must take for another life on earth.

Q. Will you explain the Great Invocation and how it came?

A. When man is purifying his thoughts, great inspiration comes from the different types of muses. The muses bring quotations to be used by repeating their wise words. Some inspiration is through music, and some is by writing. These are the interpretations of what man needs on earth. In speaking of the invocation; there are many people on earth who cannot or do not read their Bible, and do not understand it when they read it. They are given inspired words by others that will attune them to their Higher Self, and we have no objection to it.

We recommend you individually pray, "Our Father Who art in Heaven, hallowed be and glorify Thy Name." That is for your own individual expression. We have no condemnation for those who use any type of prayer. We do object to going through false movements or affirmations that you think in time may reach the God power.

Q. Could you explain the symbol of the shedding of the blood?

A. The shedding of the blood is when you give up your physical existence. It is only through your blood that sin can reveal itself to you. Through hatred, anger, passion, lust, desires and greediness, you create all diseases. To be washed by the pure blood means you must give up the world in its actions, and the pleasures that it represents in physical life.

Q. Yessue, could you speak a little of the different types of love?

A. There are many types of love. The highest type of love is of My Father which art in heaven. In those terms it means the Heavenly Father and the Father who works through flesh on earth. It also means to Almighty God. The only height you can reach is through the realms of your earth, and through the efforts of your God Mind.

When you speak of the world or people in general, you are not picking out individuals, you are speaking to the godliness in man. You are speaking on those terms to man so he may give up his selfish ways, false understanding, greed and lust for the earth and its manifestations. Let me explain that many of your mortal acts or your man-made acts on earth are pure because your mind is pure, the God Mind in you.

However, one must never get to the place where they think they are God in action. For when you do, you will fall back into earth's lessons. When you ascend, you do not know what hour of the day or night it comes. You do not know at this moment when death will arrive or when you will enter into the other invisible life. So in all things you have on earth, and in all your ways, there are two meanings. You must look for those two meanings and choose from it what you so desire.

Q. Somewhere in the Bible it says the earth will be destroyed by fire. Can you explain that?

A. It does not speak of the planet, it speaks of this earthly body. What fire is greater for purification than the tests which you go through. Fire represents purity in thought and in action. The body will represent whatever you choose to demonstrate. It is not speaking of the earth as your planet.

Q. Would You tell us where, when, and how You gave up the physical life 2000 years ago?

A. Two thousand years ago, many of you walked while I walked on earth, stepped in my footprints, and advised the troops. Some of you bear records you do not remember, but they will be revealed when you are ready. Yes, I died on the cross, as it is said. I died of the mortal self, endeavoring to explain the Truth to people living and existing on the earth at that time, that the flesh body cannot enter the Kingdom of Heaven. Your invisible body can ascend at death when the soul and your ego mind change their attitudes and become a perfect whole.

When I came on earth there was no false pretense, no glamour, and no misunderstanding. The three wise men are your three states of consciousness; there can be no other explanation for it. Born as a babe means you must begin again. I have endeavored to explain that as you grow into manhood, you pass through seven changes of life. The first seven years, you are guarded by the ones who have been put in charge of you. The second seven years is the youth interpretation of life, and much of it is misleading. The third is when man steps out into the world on his own, makes his own sin, and corrects his own sphere. When you reach the higher changes, each one will unfold, until your age of forty-nine years. If you live to be forty-nine and you have not expressed the Godliness in you, you will return to earth at death. You will then build life anew so that eventually you may ascend.

Many of you have asked, "Why Master, am I at this age and just beginning to learn." It is because you were not willing to give up the false ideas. In God's kingdom, there is no time and no age limit. Death is the only limitation that man puts upon himself. I leave you in peace. My name is Yessue Ben Miriam, in this generation where you have walked on earth with Me, that is the name I carried. Amen. Amen. Amen.

11

THE CREATIVE FORCE

"My Soul greets thee. My heart is filled with Love for all my fellowmen. My lips speak words of Truth and I give praise to God on high. Amen. Amen. Amen."

When man talks about the Creative Force, he talks about creation as if it were such a common thing that he hardly bothers with it, except to receive its conveniences. Man agrees with much he has heard about, but cannot take time from his daily habits to prove what is true to his own satisfaction. It is convenient to agree because it requires so little effort. It is not so simple or easy to put it into action.

Creative Force is everywhere and in everything. It is understood that God created everything in the beginning. But who has created since that time, how did they do it, and what is the difference?

Have you ever thought about how far away from the earth you could think about accurately? Everywhere you can look, think, see, or know is of the Creative Force. The stone, plant, animal and man are all of the Creative Force. Do you think the other creations look at you and wonder why you are different than they are, or wonder how you were created? Do you ever wonder why the other creations, year after year, never change their patterns or start making something different? It seems in all of God's creation, man is the only one that is dissatisfied with his form. If you have not thought about this force around you, then you have much to learn.

I would like you to imagine being out in space about twenty-five miles from the earth where you will find nothing but the forces. You will find it is air, wind, atmosphere, and ether, which contain heat, cold, moisture and dryness. Some call it the earth, air, water and fire elements. Many agree with this but they don't tell you what part you were created from or how your pattern is maintained year after year. Do the patterns that you see or know about ever get mixed up during their creation? Most will agree that this does not happen for each pattern takes after its own kind. But do you think about where those patterns are kept?

We agree here that man can imitate the likeness of some creating but he cannot create his own pattern. All creation is made of creative forces and contains three important ingredients. You hear from the pulpits that God is Omnipotent, Omnipresent and Omniscient. This Creator has the power to do all things according to the patterns, is everywhere present, and intelligent because It is wise and knows how to do things. Many books tell you the same thing and you accept it because you cannot prove differently. That is not thinking for yourself, that is blind faith.

Omniscient, Omnipresence, and Omnipotence are the trine, of just one part of creation, the principle. That principle is the cause behind all God's creation, as you will come to see. In fact, this principle is what you mean when you say God. God and man have never become detached or are they ever lost from one another. You are part of this Ring of Force which encircles the earth. The universe cannot be complete without you, its completeness really depends upon you.

You are right in the center of God's creation, the

center of His universal plan. We say center because Principle is God Power, reduced down in quality of His Presence so you can know and understand it as your own activity of Himself. Oh, the wonder of Its presence in you.

Now, how can you work all this Principle that is in you? You must realize that God Power is potent and was broken down so man can remain as his individual pattern. You will find three things have taken place: power, force and energy. Power is reduced into three actions as capacity, faculties, and ideas or patterns. All this is called force. Force is that part of power in you which contains compulsion or movement. Energy is a decreased strength of force which endures and holds together, therefore it is called strength.

You are the center or core of all this greatness. You are a part of the same force that compels the earth to stay in the heavens, and it compels you to stay on the earth as long as you are in this flesh body. You have this force at your command but you don't think of it unless things go wrong with your outer shell or body. Then you will turn to this Power you call God to make all things right as they were in the beginning. How patient this Great Principle is with his children.

In the Bible it tells you that the Lord God or Law, breathed the breath of life into your nostrils and made you a Living Soul. In this great force around the earth there is a substance that contains the patterns of all things on earth. This substance contains the pattern which you breathe, and this pattern cannot enter any other living thing upon the earth. The substance which belongs to man is from the Kingdom of the Twelve Great Workers of Power known as the Gods. This substance is called prana. This prana is your spirit which means absolute energy, the vital force, the essence of life. Wherever there is life there is prana, because without it, there is nothing but space.

In the atom, electron, ion, and the common grain of sand there is prana. The Bible tells you to seek the Lord, and the Lord of your universe is this principle of the prana in you. It is only by seeking and feeling this Lord that you will receive understanding. This is the marriage that is written of in the Bible and is the Law that Moses spoke about that you should not adulterate. Take time to think about the meanings in the Bible and about the Ten Commandments. This lesson has great value, and I place it into your hands with great love, so that you may know the greatness of God in every man.

Man's creation is threefold: animal nature, mortal nature and a spiritual nature. This simply means his productive force, vital force and prana force, or again energy, force and power. You are in this great sea of force around the earth and you cannot change it, but you can let it change you. It does not matter what names are given to these things as long as you know the meaning and place where they belong.

The flesh body is real to you because you can see and feel its substance as your outer expression. You cannot see yourself think, but you can accept the principle that you do. You cannot see Thoughts, but you can know and accept that Thoughts are things and are abundant around you. You cannot see great ideas which are everywhere, yet you accept that some intelligent people receive them. You stand in the center of all power, force and energy as life. Man is willing to accept the effect of life more readily than the cause of life.

The Soul uses energy to manifest the physical law as matter substance, mind substance and vital substance. Each of these three uses of energy are equally distributed and at man's disposal.

The first energy of life to study is the vital energy and is before you in your daily existence. This vital substance is your sex energy. It is the only part of you in which the positive and negative forces are composed of the same substance and from the same force, but different in action. The positive force is the incoming energy force and the negative force is the outgoing energy force. One you call death and one you call life. One effect you can see and one you do not see.

Your sexual energy is the God Principle in you, and it holds the image of God Thy Father. How degraded the man of the pulpit would feel as he stands before his congregation and speaks of God in you, if he understood that he was speaking of your sex force energy. Your sexual energy is the creator working within you.

After birth a child's body grows to become the user of sexual energy. From the first sexual experience the human being actually enters upon a program of physical destruction. Every time the act occurs, there is an expenditure of vital forces, whose presence within the human body make it a thing Divine. To make this act meet the approval of the neighbors, man marries, not to please God Principle, but for race progeny. It is common understanding among all races of people, that life is one sexual experience after another, called sexual intercourse. If you are married before your friends or neighbors, your intercourse is Godly. Otherwise, in the public eye, you are sinners. Where I ask, have you placed God?

The sexual act, in itself, is not necessarily something that makes you good or evil, or brings great joy. Rarely do you find anyone who has reached that beautiful superconscious understanding that it should become. Here we come to the acknowledgment that the act itself is not evil, but the thought behind the act makes it evil.

It is commonly known in your medical profession that it is not necessary to perform sexual intercourse. Many others believe, for various reasons, that the sexual act hinders their progress because of their religious view, disdain, or belief they are more pious when they abstain from the expression of intercourse. They are in the same category as those who lack the opportunity, but the expression of the thought is there just the same.

The constant thinking about sexual expression, not the lack of expression, brings about disease. You must rise not only above the act, but learn to turn your thinking away from the act by knowing the true cause of the act. Many who do not express sexually find trials of peculiar irritability and restlessness, followed by physical lassitude, mental disturbance and probable seriously ill health. This is felt so strongly today that medical science declares that practically all disease is traceable to an unsatisfied or repressed sex life. This results in many physical conditions such as constipation as the beginning of many serious and lingering diseases, mental trouble common because of the selfish natures of man today, and some forms of eye trouble caused by the hidden reflections of thinking about excessive or repressed sexual acts.

I do not tell you only about the physical side of sex, nor do I mean to dwell too long upon the act. Since its fundamental principle is the cause of its function, it is best to understand it. There is nothing to be ashamed about in sex activity, unless it is in the thinking. In the justification of sex energy let me again say that all energy is sex energy. As you are able to build a new body each time you re-enter in the evolution of life on earth, you are also able to repair this body when it becomes ill, in distress or broken down with age. In the very act of calling your inner Chemist for repairs, you put into action your sex energy substance. The only difference is that you put your action of thinking on cleanliness.

As I taught man to turn within to find the Truth, it also applies to this part of life. Man must be strong enough to meet this Truth face to face. Until he does, he can do nothing about his life in regard to becoming a normal spiritual man.

Now let us turn toward the servant of God. If the servant of God is the server of God and man, then we must turn to the sex energy to get this great understanding. The human body is the servant through which all energy must pass. The sex energy must first pass through your first nerve center called the chakra in some teachings. Then the mind energy, your thinking energy, directs it to either the higher level of life, or the act of intercourse, either revealed or hidden. The conscious act is where the conscience sets the Law of Effect.

There is a way to know this body divinely and to feel the subtle forces at work within you. You can watch them at work within yourself or others, but you must study to know the scheme of things around and within you. The forces of energy in man can open the door of light by the faculties of Intuition and Inspiration. Man may approach sexual relationships in a lewd and coarse manner, crushing the highest inspiration that can come consciously to him, wasting his substance in licentious and ugly passion, even to taking a life. Children of light, as you journey upon your path of light, do not be afraid of God's forces in you, but seek to understand them. You need not condone evil actions of passion, but do not condemn those who do not understand its right use.

The Law of Nature is absolute, unchangeable, immutable and irrevocable. Your mind is the power which guides, directs, controls and governs the use of Universal Forces, Mind Substances and Vital Energy. One finds great understanding when he fathoms these words in their true sense: Law, Principle, Mind and

Energy Substance when used as the infinite and universal application to all things, persons, and conditions, limited only in use by man himself.

As you seek to know your own Law, the Lord of your universe, it is important to know and remember the endocrine glands and their effect upon the human body. Microcosm means man and macrocosm refers to the universe. It is the dual nature that is meant to express: one within man and one outside of man.

Within man the nature energies are carried through the ductless glands, which is the contact between God and man through the nervous system. This contact is governed through man by the ductless endocrine glands and these glands are the makers of man's destiny. Your Chemist works to build up, sustain and maintain your body through the endocrine glands and they make no selection of people as to the station in life, high or low, good or evil. It does not define your fame, beauty, strength or age, crippled or straight; all these things only show that your endocrine glands have made it so. It does not define those of different skin colors, or those virtuous or unvirtuous; they are all the same to the endocrine glands. The currents and undercurrents that go on through the Chemist of your body help to build up or break down, and change the body from youth to old age; all are the work of your endocrine glands.

The Archangel Kingdom determines all changes that are worked out through your gland systems. It is important to know and understand the glands of your physical body. To be a Spiritual Being you must learn how to use what the Gods have deemed it right to use, or how can you evolve?

The master glands, called the gonad vital organs or sex glands, are the first glands to learn about. They are directly and sympathetically related to all other glands. Injury to them will cause injury to the whole body.

When they are depleted, run down or exhausted, the whole body suffers. All human energy is related to sex energy and without it there is no beauty, no sheen or quality to the skin, and no strength. It is very noticeable that no genius is found among those who are depleted in this energy. You will also find no genius in men who have been castrated or women who have had their ovaries removed. Reactions become sluggish and heavy, women grow masculine in appearance and the voice looses its sweetness or key pitch.

Certain orders or cults believe in suppression of sex energy only to discover that men become feminine in their actions or work, and the women become masculine in actions and appearance. Take into consideration that if they had good spiritual or healthy education on this subject, much of the transformation of character traits need not occur. It should be clear to the right thinking person that the creative force of Spirit sends the life stream through these organs to perpetuate the life of the universe.

We have heard many students say pertaining to the physical study of man, that they already know this and are looking for something higher to Mastership. Seekers of Light, I urge you to reconsider such statements, for there is surely something you have overlooked in reading or hearing this work. You have passed over one of the most important things to make your life a perfect whole. One must not only receive knowledge but he must use that knowledge. I ask you again to go over these words so you may receive help from the Masters as they try to help you fulfill your life pattern.

The Gonad glands in the male are the testicles and in the female are the ovaries. They are the most delicate, yet most marvelously complex set of glands in the human system, or of the ductless glands. The secretion in the male is positive and called spermatozoa, and in the female it is negative and called ova. Remember it is through these glands that the foundation substance or secretion forms a human body in the womb. Surely you realize it contains the Divine Power and origin of life. Since man was made by God in the beginning, and the stream of life has always flowed, you could understand to what great extent that God knew His plans. He has caused thousands of changes to take place, passing through thousands of people, so that you may be where you are right now.

In the male the gonads have a dual natural action, as inner and outer. It is to this hidden action that man owes all his success in the business world, as well as his appearance to the people in general. It is this inner secretion that is poured into the bloodstream of his body as vital, valuable internal fluids. They make the light in his eye that he calls sight, the elastic spring in his step, the melody in his voice and gives charm to his personality. To be considered beyond all this, is the Glory Crown of Light or Aura that is often seen around the head of man.

The male is more conscious of his sex energy than the female because he is both positive and negative, while a female is only negative. Since mankind has been created as both Spiritual and mortal being, we will place each organ action with the body that it functions in. The gonads are the principle gland action in the physical body. It is the most important function in the race evolution. The gonads have a direct connection with the spiritual man or being, but this takes place in the physical body's glandular system.

The pineal gland is the most important gland in the spiritual man. We shall refer to this gland as the Center of Centers. The secretion of this gland is positive. It is above the pituitary gland in the human head. This gland known all through man's evolution, has been called the Seat of Man's Soul. We agree Soul means Mind, the God Mind. It is referred to as the All Seeing Eye, especially in occult study. The name is not as important as to understand its action.

The Golden Cord is attached to this pineal gland. If it is touched in any way, death will result. It is through the Golden Cord at the top of the head that all spiritual energies enter man, and they are only positive in action. It is when this positive secretion meets the vital energy from the physical body that man becomes illumined. You can see then, how important it is for the vital sex energy force of inner action to turn upward from the solar plexus center to meet the Spiritual Force or energy which passes down to the vital organ of the heart. Each energy which enters the body, both of the visible and invisible action has a center from which it sends energy to a vital organ that it works through.

The center for Spiritual Energy is the pineal gland and its vital organ is the heart. The Vital Energy's center is the solar plexus and the Sex energy's organ is the gonads. One more thing we will call to your attention: in the female the gonads are closely connected with the mammary and thyroid glands. Amen. Amen. Amen.

Aura Chart

1 **Human Aura**	2 **Mortal Aura**	3 **Divine Aura**
Mental Mind.	Faculty Mind.	God Will Mind
Mortal Will.	Faculty Will.	Conception Will
Thinking	Thought.	Idea
Shape.	Pattern.	Formula

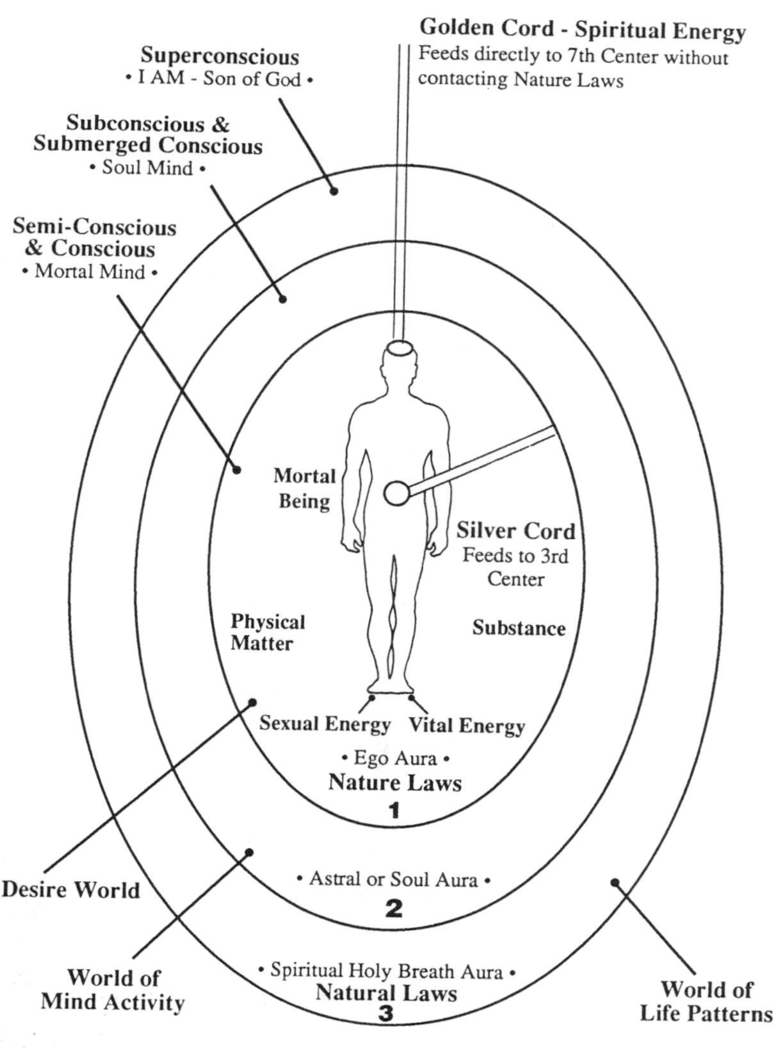

The Twelve Faculties

God Mind Faculties
Crown of Glory
Natural Laws

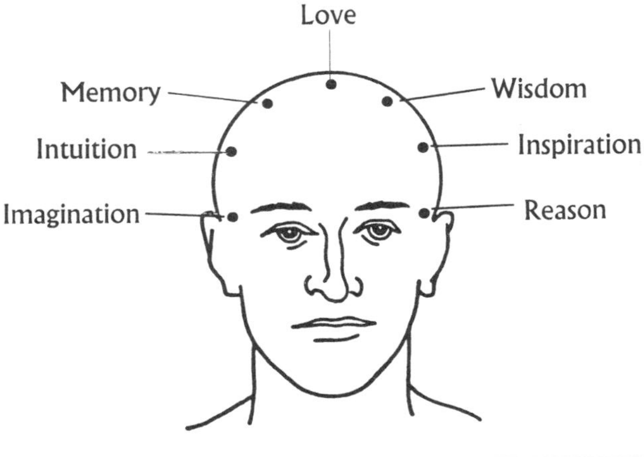

Five Physical Senses
Nature Laws

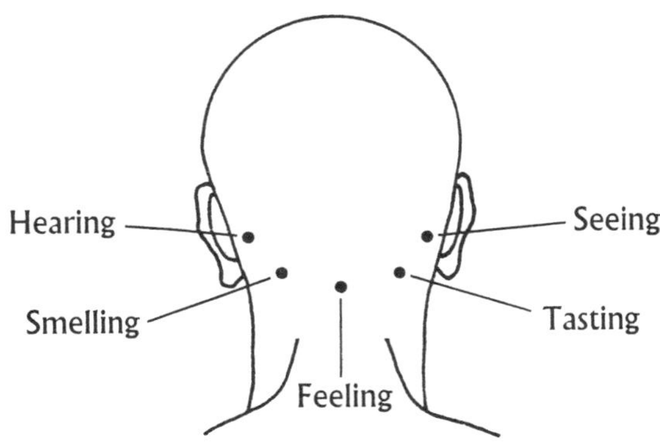

These sense buds are under the skull bone
in the soft part of the membrane

Nerve Centers

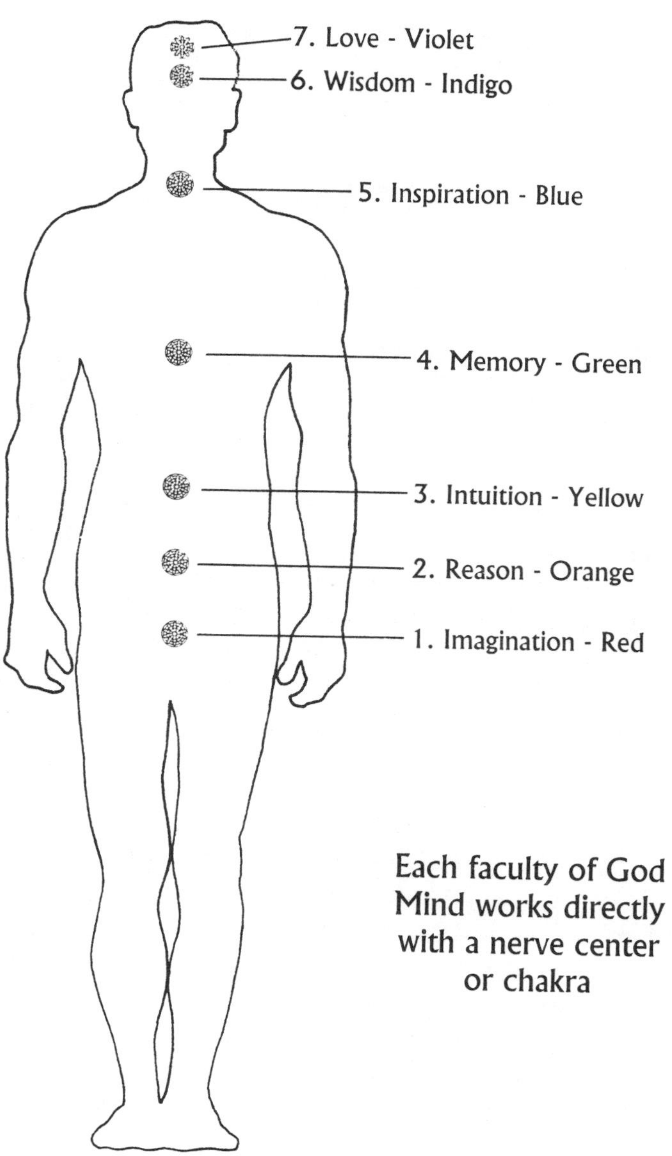

Each faculty of God Mind works directly with a nerve center or chakra

12

HEAL THYSELF

The following chapters are given by the Ascended Masters who are the twelve councilors of the Radiant Temple within Mt. Shasta. This Council works under the direction of their Elder Brother, Yessue Ben Miriam.

"I give to you the greetings of the Great White Brotherhood from the Radiant Temple of Mt. Shasta. I give this greeting because it connects the invisible spaces that are around you, with your Thought Form. My Soul greets thee. My heart is filled with Love for all fellowmen. I shall speak words of Truth, giving praise to God on high. Amen. Amen. Amen."

Around each mortal human being is an individual aura. It is constructed to fit the type of physical thinking body and a God Mind. It forms the pattern that the mortal human being uses while on earth. The first aura around the physical body is the physical aura. This aura is next to the body and is usually red in color. It is constructed to absorb the nature energies needed to function the physical body. These energies are used by man within every twenty-four hour period of his aura cycle.

The color red attracts the type of physical energies needed in each human body. We call it a magnetic field.

It is the field that attracts from the ethers, the exact type of atoms or elements needed for the mental faculties and the construction of your physical body. Then the force of energy from the earth is added to awaken it and put life into each particle absorbed in the system.

Many people through breathing, thinking, inactivity, or over-activity either misuse or do not use, much of the energy sent to build the body and mind into a perfect form. Notice I do not use the word "body" I said, "form." The body I refer to consists of your flesh form and the aura around it. Then you would speak of it as a body. The stimulation of the magnetic field awakens the five physical senses. This is the other part or another form making the two in one.

If anyone who has a perfect contact with their God mind, should by their thinking activity of desires, appetites, or habits of any kind, even for one moment, change their thinking capacity from perfection, they cannot draw into their body the good atoms. Then they have no picture of perfection upon it, and in time, year after year, month after month, or even day after day, find that great damage can be done to the pattern of the form.

Mentally, every cell in the brain matches the cells or sections of your body. It is the thinking that quickens the cells into activity. So when inactive or wrong pictures are placed on the cells of the brain, the order is directed according to the picture on the brain cell and that is where the damage is done.

Those who just seek relief from pain or sickness, but do not desire to do their own thinking, are only seeking the apparent relief of pain. Because people are not anxious to remove the underlying cause of the pain it has brought about many of the different types of healing. We call these the compounds and liquids of medicine, the magnetic touch of the hands, or some form of what is commonly called magic powers. It is only for relief from pain. Sometimes, the feeling of gratitude for the relief of pain or the removal of fear, will remove the cause. However, until the cause is removed from the aura, there is no healing, only relief.

Referring to the acts Yessue Ben Miriam performed on earth, He taught His disciples that the cause underlying all acts of healing was elimination of the destructive action of thinking. Healing removed fear, doubt and opened the eyes so that they could behold their Higher Self. He showed the disciples that it was possible for Him to tell exactly what someone needed. To some He said, "Go and sin no more." Did that mean they were physically misusing the energies, or did it refer to their evil thinking and the misuse of their imagination pictures? Did they have thought pictures of greed, hate, vanity or passion ruling their life? When He said, "Go and sin no more," He meant they must change their thinking. He told them they must see clearly, and to see clearly, they must understand.

To others, there was a cause of death in motion and apparently the cause of death was set aside. For when He said, "Arise and be sound," it meant they must have the desire to live life, and that was the awakening. They needed the desire to fulfill their pattern, have courage about their earth life, and be willing to accept the spiritual life pattern through the earth pattern.

There were those who were eaten up with disease, deformity, and many other actions that are beyond the word illness. He saw their thoughts of destruction, their enmity against others, their dishonor for the word of others, and their greed for what must be earned by work. They had the desire of taking without work. He saw their belief that the great powers had no effect on them. Because they believed wealth or possessions were higher than man, they did not see the possibilities that God could reach them.

To some, this Great God of Understanding gave the type of lesson that would unfold their thinking ability. Without the use of their thinking ability, they had no way to contact the higher source of invisible life. Therefore, His first manifestation was to change their way of thinking, to erase ignorance from their state of consciousness, and place in it the true picture of living life. He created a great desire in them for a useful life, instead of their beggarly acts.

Blessed are they who seek the Law of God. Blessed are they who serve in the name of Lord God. Truly if you were to dissect your physical body and see the contacts of your higher bodies in this one form, you would understand what I am saying. You stand in the presence of the God over your life, and you work in His presence, for that presence is within.

As you step forward in life, know that God will walk with you, stand with you, and serve with you. That is all your thoughts need to be concerned with. Do not allow yourself to be disturbed with what others think about you. Let your thoughts of the wholeness of love remove all physical acts, words, and deeds of mortal man. When you can talk with yourself by spoken words, often you will hear the answer within. No physical, human, mental mind, can stop thinking and remain a living example of life.

We teach you as students of light to learn to meditate. When you meditate, sit down and endeavor not to think of your work of the day, your money, possessions, or your lack or fulfillment of anything. We endeavor to get you to relax into nothingness, and if you do, then you will return to the pureness of your pattern. With your effort, each time you may unfold more and more. You learn not to interfere with the works of God.

If a man stood before you with leprosy, you would not notice it; only God and the man would know what is wrong and you would bless it. You would see that his pattern needs to be fulfilled, for nothing stops until the pattern has been completed.

It has always been the effort of our teaching to stop criticism and condemnation of the self, and to bring all of the sins or the wrongness of the pattern to your Godhead within. Then there is no secret undissolved, or no miracles performed for your acclamation. What has taken place must first take place within the mind quality of man, before it reacts on the body.

When a man has suffered long and has been tormented by fears and doubts of a disease, it means that his body is being dissolved or destroyed. If he does nothing to cleanse his mind's thinking power and his acts by his own willpower, then nothing can be done for him. If a man has suffered long and desires to find his freedom, he will bring himself before the God in himself. If he is willing to turn it all over to God, accept his pain, discomfort, and accept a change by death, he has surrendered his earthly desires of control. He has given all to the Higher Power to be or do whatever is required. Then that man is ready for what is called a miracle healing, but it is not a miracle. The healing takes place because there is nothing left to be removed.

As a healer, if you use magnetic healing to instill your energy, you are imposing your type of life energies into another aura. When you impose your energies or magnetic activity of energy, you are imposing your type of hormones into their pattern of life. If they are lacking in positive energies, and you impose your type of energies into them, it may happen to be positive. You will then create either more, or an opposite pattern of what their type requires. No two males are alike; no two females are alike; each body is required to carry a certain amount of energies. When they consume all of one type and do not use the other type, and you impose your type on them, you are creating a confused life. This is an adultery of the mixing of energies and there is no earthly power that will remove the cause behind their condition.

We often tell students that around each part of your body, such as the glands, vital organs, and nerve centers, there is a veil. In the Bible it is written of as the veil, which is a sheath. When the heavy use of nicotine or alcohol takes place, it destroys one or more of the sheaths. If it is the sheath around a vital organ that is destroyed, such as the heart, liver, stomach, spleen, or any vital part, that part or organ is open to disease. There is no way that disease gets into your body except through the destruction of the sheath in some way.

Disease differs from illness or sickness; it is not and never has been the same. When any sheath around the centers is affected, you have a nervous disorder in the body. Many different actions may result, such as, retarded actions of any of the organs or centers, or the brain faculties. When man is in complete working order and is not absorbing nicotine, is not a heavy drinker, and is absent from destructive action, he can have free thinking will in action. Free thinking will gives man the ability to gradually go a step higher in learning, not accepting more than he can understand.

A man who accepts the higher spiritual work and neglects his physical body, has nothing to store away, and no place to hold the records. Therefore, his memory will slowly but surely diminish causing an ill effect on his mentality and understanding. His pattern is then neglected and incomplete at death.

We advise every student to search and seek gradually. He does not need to ask for everything to be explained as he is used to. Endeavor to accept what is said and make the effort to understand it. When man asks for Truth, and then tells those who bring Truth to him how he wants it, he is not seeking Truth. He is following his own pattern which he idolizes. Ask for Truth, but do not ask for the way you want or desire it to be given. Amen. Amen. Amen.

13

THE SENSE OF FEELING

"My Soul greets thee. My heart is filled with Love for all fellowmen. I shall speak words of Truth, giving praise to God on high. Amen, Amen, Amen."

When we speak or use the language that you are acquainted with, it is a picture that is reflected upon the center which reflects from the fourth, fifth, sixth, and seventh dimensions. The words that are spoken are the reflection of what is explainable to anyone in the languages that are being used.

If an entity or a departed spirit takes possession of a person who channels, shutting off their mental intelligence so the nerve connection of action is not under control of their own individual mental mind, this entity will speak in the language that they understand. Sometimes, it is called "talking in tongues." If you have friends or acquaintances who speak more than one or two languages, then you can understand it would be quite easy for an entity to express in languages that they are acquainted with.

When our work is done by mental reflection through an instrument, it works through the veil of imagination or reflection. For instance, if we wanted a tree to be described, a picture of a tree is reflected into the instrument's mental mind. If the mental mind is stilled, it functions as any sense activity would, and the instrument would use their own words to explain the picture. Signs and symbols are the language of the Soul. We endeavor to explain why the true reflection is reflected in every man's consciousness if he will permit it. We desire to show you how to use your fifth sense, the sense of feeling, and how to understand it.

While many people upon the earth go about in groups and talk of peace and love, they do not know what they are speaking about. I am not saying they do not think they know, because they do think they know, but, in reality, it does not come close to the Truth. Man has five physical senses. He believes he hears and is able to denote what the sound means. If he hears the knock of a hammer or ring of a bell, he believes he can tell what it is. He says it is his hearing but hearing is only the resounding board of sound. The actual hearing is feeling, the fifth sense. When you hear a sound, listen to whether it is loud or soft, a harsh or sweet-tone, or what it sounds like. Your sense of feeling is what appreciates the sound.

Your sense of feeling is not only in the ears. Your ear only contacts the sounds or rates of vibration in the third and a small part of the fourth dimension. The sense of feeling is heard all over and felt throughout your body, until it is recognized by your mental mind. Then your hearing tells you what you think you hear.

When you use your sense of smell, you cannot tell what it is without your sense of feeling working. If you taste, your taste buds work with the sense of feeling. There are many who do not have the sense of taste. The sense of sight only sees the outer surface of things, but your inner feeling tells you what can happen from what you see. It can tell you what will become of it by what you see. The sense of feeling is the contact with your conscious state of existence.

Very little has been told about the fifth sense of

feeling which belongs to your physical world. Feeling also contacts the part within you which contacts the higher worlds and your higher faculties. We are going to take the sense of consciousness apart and show you how to put it together again, because you use it everyday. The sense of consciousness, the awareness, is all you are able to use in your physical world. When man understands this, he will then depend more upon his impressions, urges, hunches, and his psychic force, because the higher consciousness does not work with the obstacles on earth or the visible world.

Many of the great teachers have neglected to teach what the stages of consciousness are. They divide it into the subconscious, meaning the hidden consciousness. They also teach, in some instances, that there is a submerged consciousness. They will tell you there is a super consciousness, and only when you reach that point can you really call yourself "saved." I ask you, saved from what? It will not save you from death, if that is what they understand. Only when you learn how to overcome death will you ever be able to do that act.

When they speak of the subconscious mind, they refer to those things that do not work with objects or things that are used in the physical earth world. They mean that which is before the object as pattern, intention, or plan, and the good or evil it works. When they speak of their submerged consciousness, they refer to the patterns of all the lives they have lived while upon this earth, and some can go farther back than that. No matter how far back you may go in knowing your life patterns, that will not save you.

Any student or physical teacher upon the earth who believes they can avoid the hard effort of work to reach higher and higher, by individual effort, while in the physical body, does not work with the Truth. It is only when you begin to experience opposition, temptations, an aching heart, suffering, lost friends, and the loss of your physical possessions, that you ever come through the training that brings you to the higher step or the place where you are called resurrected.

The Christ Man, who claimed that He came to teach mankind, taught all that I speak of. He taught what man must pass through to recognize the value of his Higher Self, which is the only God Self he will ever know. It does not matter whether you call it your Christ Self, the I Am self, or your Holy Spirit. The intention of your great desire for the glories of the heavens can produce what many words and intentions spoken by man on earth cannot produce.

Now getting back to the intentions of your five physical senses. There are many teachers meeting the public today, who endeavor to teach their students to forget their physical self and apply all their intention to the Higher Self. I speak with no disrespect toward any other teacher or student. I am stating a clear and precise fact; you cannot forget this body, the action of your physical senses, or the educational training in this physical life. It is impossible to reach your Soul activity any other way than through your mental mind. Mind controls the physical senses or physical body; either by the will of man, or the will of God. One means man's will of experience, and the other is God's will to cure man by removing all that hinders him.

Let us suppose that a man came to earth with much evil to overcome. Call it sin, error or karma, it makes no difference. He comes with an evil pattern. It is a great sin to teach man to avoid the conditions that bring about his opportunity to be tested. Anyone who interferes with another man's pattern will take on his karma. That is why there are many on this earth today that suffer with more than they can bear, because they carry other loads that do not belong to them.

That is why, in families upon this earth, every child should be taught principles of right from wrong. Every child should be taught to stand upon his own decisions, accepting whatever good comes, or whatever he thinks or sees as evil to come. That does not mean that parents should abuse their children with unnatural punishment. We do not mean that at all. But when parents of today, say "No", they do not mean it. They will eventually give in and add more to it. The child does not know what to depend on, look up to, or respect.

It is our endeavor to teach both parents and students, wherever they are, and whenever they come, to recognize the highest aspects of their five physical senses. When they do that, they will open the door to the higher mind faculties. When the state of consciousness is deepened, instead of taking things apart, they can see the reason and the function behind all these things. Then they are ready for higher work. It will help them understand, and not detract from them.

There are certain persons upon this earth that some students or people might say are chosen ones. Even in your schools, there are those that are called the teacher's favorite ones. That is not true in working with the Master's teachings. The student that seems to receive the least attention, seems slower in gaining his aspirations, and sometimes seems to go through harder tasks and temptation, feels the harshness of the world attention, and experiences the falseness of friends; all these are his stepping stones. He may be higher spiritually than those who stand and preach or seem to be the chosen ones.

If all the tasks placed before man are easily performed, with nothing to overcome, no plan or task that requires effort, then he feels he is gone or lost. When man accepts any task that is put before him, he needs to take the thorns as well as the flowers. He takes the heat of suffering, as well as the comforts of life. All this is put before man to test him, to cause him to aspire and to believe with a dependable belief. He cannot have faith one day and then wonder the next day. This is not a dependable attitude in the testing of man. If your task is put before you to accomplish and you are not told how it is to be done, rest assured that they have ascertained your ability, your mental capacity, and your testing ground, to see that you will carry it through.

We often read in the Bible and in other records that pre-date the Bible; that he who follows in the footsteps of the Masters and the great teachers, will find a stony path. He will find coldness in the world, and attract less attention, until he despairs of ever doing anything worthwhile. Cannot man realize, this is the building of ground? If a man was in the midst of a body of water and did not know how to reach the shore, is there not something in him that tells him, "Try! try! you can if you will. We will help you." Yet, if the man will not make the effort, he will never reach the shore. Although, he may tell many people, before this experience, that he has faith and believes in the Higher Power, but when he is put to the test he cannot produce a result.

There are times that you sway. One hour you wonder, "How is it all going to come out?" The next minute, "I am sure it will." A little later on, "I wonder if this is the best way? Should I have changed something? Can I depend upon this?" You cannot depend upon any object. You must depend on your Higher Self which is your God Self. It is the only POWER you have in your body. Otherwise, you have all force and energy. Force will only work with that which it came to work for; the negative and positive forces that build and contain this life as a pattern. The force you use and have left over in your body is a magnetic attraction or a magnetic field, that attracts the sound belt which carries Thought.

The power that comes to man, through his higher centers, does not come with any physical attraction at all. It is the product of man's God Will to be the overcomer; to speak with few words, and yet carry a great message. Plant a seed here and a seed there as words of wisdom. If the seeds you plant are not accepted, they are not forgotten. In another life someone may find their way through those seeds you planted.

If Thoughts are pictures of objects, called prana objects, reflected upon your invisible mirror or imagination, then what is the recognition of your higher sense, the Higher Self or the I AM? It is not excluded from the physical earth life and objects, or ways of life, for they contain it all. Here is where man departs from the Truth and depends upon his own ego, or his thinking ability of the objects of earth. You cannot do anything in the physical world without contacting an object.

We realized long ago that this way of teaching Christian philosophy would not be an easy task. Without flaunting the ego before man, it holds no great attraction. We have told everyone, it would be a task to serve, but when you seek and serve, the answer will come. We have shown you that life can go up and it can go down. As long as there is prosperity, then things are very happy, and seem easy to do. Intentionally, when supplies go down, man begins to ponder and take things apart, and wonder how God can master the situation.

Do you recall the Bible story when Elisha was called to the widow's home? She had no means of support or food supply. She did not have the supply of oil, which her husband had been able to use to manage his living expenses. Elisha told her to bring all the empty vessels that she could find and he would fill them with oil, and he did. Then, he told her to go borrow from her neighbors all the available containers. She did and Elisha filled them with oil. Her faith before was empty, but after she "saw" the supply, she was thrilled into the great action of faith and belief. If you could have followed that story, when she was selling the supply for her means of livelihood, it went down, until the vessels became empty again, because she did not have the faith.

So the testing ground is to receive your supply, and if you lose it, you must make a decision what you are going to do about it. Are you going to believe in the objects you see, or are you going to believe in the prana, which you do not see? Faith is the substance from which all things are created. Faith then is prana in the physical world. I am hoping you listen and think over the words of wisdom that have been given to you here. Amen. Amen. Amen.

14

SOURCE OF LIFE

"I give to you the greetings of the Great White Brotherhood. My Soul greets thee. My heart is filled with Love for all fellowmen. I shall speak words of Truth, giving praise to God on High. Amen. Amen. Amen."

How long will it take man to realize that the records of the Holy Bible were never meant to be taken as a religion. Many of those records were made hundreds of years after any occurrence was recorded in your Bible. The older records were made in such a crude manner that much was lost. The records of the New Testament were made close to four hundred years after the birth of the man honored as Jesus the Christ.

Now as you look back four hundred years, your history experts called scientists, do much research to go back four hundred years. Very few of your actual records of the history of the United States can go back more than two hundred years. Is it any wonder that the people have misunderstood and have been misguided by the records of the Bible.

We do not criticize nor condemn the religions. They have kept man in a civilized state of mind, so that he could build his faith into something he did not see or hold, and that would help him live a cleaner life. But, for a religion to teach such mistaken activities, and found a spiritual Truth on it, man will eventually know he has been misled, which takes away all the good that has been done.

For hundreds of years, those who reigned as spiritual leaders of Christian life taught man the things that he should worship. Now man is finding there never were such things. That is why the people of today, all over your earth, are turning away from the things that have held many generations together. We have endeavored to slowly break through this wall of ignorance. It has not been the easiest duty to perform from any of the Temples.

Everywhere upon the earth, in every language or race we have worked with, we have endeavored to take out the falseness and give actual facts of Truth. I say facts, because these facts can be proven, as far as your material understanding goes. In many cases, breaking down the wall built up around our Elder Brother, Yessue Ben Miriam, has been the hardest wall to get over. A Christ man did live, work, administer, teach, and exemplify a Christian life. We agree, that man's memory of this should exist on your earth, through all the years, until man leaves the earth.

We say, the idea that one man and woman lived in a time that is called the beginning is ridiculous in its conception. How can man be considered a great scientist, know all the languages, have the records, and still believe that all the peoples upon the earth today started from one man and woman? Religions teach that God did not love Adam and Eve and cast them out. You do not do that today, most assuredly, if there was a God that created Adam and Eve, He certainly would not have let anyone do that to His Firstborn.

I ask all of you to be careful of the concepts you form of what took place in the past, because it can hold you down in ignorance. Even one little part of that ignorance can blotch your whole life. I ask you to read your Bible, it is true, but I ask you to read it with understanding. Don't take it back to the ancient age called your past, but bring it up to date, to the time you live now. It will work just as well today as it did thousands of years ago.

It has been said many are looking for the coming of the Christ. It is a story that has been told so often. Christ is already here, and has never been absent, but there will come a time when people can see Him and hear His voice. There is great misunderstanding about the Christ being born again. He is born with every child that is born, but if he does not live, that is another thing. One of the great leaders of your country said these words, "It is like a man running after a streetcar while he is on it." That was told about a man in New York many years ago, and if it was good then, it is good now. Read your Bible, but relate it to the present day. See that you understand the words, and if you don't, it is time that you looked them up. It is good for you to use your imagination, for if you cannot see what is invisible, you will never see it visibly, and you would not understand it if you did come across it.

There has been a Christ man on earth in every two thousand year period, from the time the Israel have been on earth. Every two thousand years, the Christ man has appeared where it was most acceptable, and left a record for man to follow. Your history or your records of philosophy, have told of the different ages, and have given you the names that were used at that time. You will find they did not tack on the word Jesus, or Christ, but similar activities were used.

Now you are looking for a new Christ to come on earth, and there is no new Christ. The Christ Man will come upon the earth, and will walk and talk with many of you. He will walk among you, and bless you, and teach you. I cannot say He will be in the presence of all, for there are many people on this earth. If He should appear at one place, or in a few places, and leave you records, then you can be assured it will reach and live another two thousand years for those who are going to be on earth after you are gone.

I find it is difficult for students to see and understand what is meant by the realms, and by the planes in each one of those realms. I cannot see anything that should puzzle or disturb you by using these word terms, because in your daily contact among your friends and neighbors you can see how they think. It may be beyond what you are able to think, or below what you are using as your Thought. So it is in all cases among those on earth; some are capable of reaching out and thinking about things that have never been known on your earth. There are others, even though they look at a thing, cannot think about it, nor can they describe its purpose or use. You find all types of people, some will take the wrong meaning of what that is said.

No matter how many hear the Christ who comes to earth, whether it is visible or invisible; the spoken word; or the wave length of signs, symbols, or conditions; man must make the best out of it. You should not pick it up and say, "That's it", and not struggle to find out what is behind it. What is the meaning that you do not see, but you know is there? You will find when you are too busy to listen for Truth, then you have no room for God, and God has not much room for you.

Jesus spoke to his disciples and crowds of people and said, "There will be many who will say Lord, Lord, in the end days, but I shall know them not." It is taught in your religions that forgiveness is one of the greatest principles man can use for his salvation, or to teach others for their salvation. I will say, "Do not believe you can live your life in sin, shame, or discrepancies of

Truth with no restitution. You cannot just suddenly say, "God forgive me, my sins are washed away, for that is a promise I have read in the Bible", and expect no correction. Every man will pay the price of his sins. Perhaps you sin in one way, and it will not be the same price as someone else, even though it may be similar. It is the cause, the interpretation, and the intention behind what you do that makes or destroys sin.

For you who feel religion is such a great thing, you can do as you please, and in a few days when the doctors have pronounced you incurable you can say, "I lay all my sins away. They are washed in the blood of the lamb. I am whiter than snow", will have a sad awakening. When you get over to the other side, if you go into spiritland, regardless of what realm or plane you are on, you will find whatever you have done wrong must be made right. If it is not possible to make things right from there, if it is something that has been done to someone else, and you cannot undo what has been done wrong, surely you will come back and work out that problem to its last jot.

No price is ever paid that is not deserved: it is always earned. No work is ever too great, for working it out is the only way you will ever earn your salvation. The words, "Forgive, and be made whole and clean" were intended so that your conscience would let you know you are wrong in your efforts, words, or actions. The moment you are aware of your error, it is a sin until you do something about it. It is a greater sin when you know and do nothing about it.

Even though it is said, "Ignorance is not an excuse", I will differ in this regard. If you are ignorant of what is right or wrong, or ignorant that you have done something wrong, then there was no intention in doing that wrong, and it has not become a fixed thing. The moment you become aware that you are out of line, out of the way of Truth in expression, without forgiveness, or have no patience for greater understanding, then you must make it right. Truth must come first in your own understanding. You must take it all apart if necessary, to get a clear version of it. Then if you need to ask for forgiveness for being ignorant, you are forgiven when you recognize what is true.

The sin is greater when you know and pay no heed to it. The sin is greater when you intend to harm, mislead, cause confusion or worry. The sin is greater when you know and do nothing about it. It is quite true that great sins have been committed in the physical life pattern, and if you do something about them, they can be cleared before you pass into another form. That is forgiveness, and that is washing sins in the blood of the lamb. The Truth is, blood is the life and lamb is the Thoughts. The living Thoughts purify and make all whole.

You do not have to kill a lamb, or wash anything in the blood that is life, as you commonly refer to it. Washed in the blood, while you are alive with pure Thoughts, is forgiveness to oneself. That is why there is confusion. Religions often put up a false impression of the unstable or the unnatural, which is adulterated by the impression of what is not true.

Let us look at the word "adultery" for a moment, as I have just used it. There are more false impressions about that word than there are about man or woman. What is adultery? It means: not perfect, not whole. Until you know you have done your best, and advanced as far as you are able to understand, only then can you remove adultery from your life. Adultery also means mixing the blood patterns of the races and we do not advocate that. We do not believe that anyone can mix their blood pattern and bring out a perfect whole. It has not been done yet, and we do not believe it ever will be.

We are given our work to do on this earth, and our

instructions come from the Melchizedek order, which is under the great God power. It has been given to us to undo as much as we can of the false teaching of the Bible. Every language has its Bible, every country has its Bible, and very few of them have the same intention, impression, or the knowledge as it really is.

I am going to expand a little about your earth, your universe, and the Gods that were given charge over this earth, as Gods have been given charge over many planets. Let us say that this earth sits in its universal space or earth universe. This earth, in its universe, sits in a galaxy of great stars. If you took the time to study and understand the pattern of the stars in your galaxy, you would find the Gods rule from there. They rule through their messengers that come to earth. This God power is the first belt of your universal cosmic ether. It is called cosmic because it is the beginning of the earth universe. Try to understand, those powers are coming from the great stars of the galaxy. Each God came from a certain portion of the galaxy and all His help and helpers, come from that field you call the galaxy. The twelve Gods that rule the earth made the power of cosmic ether that is around your earth, and those powers are twelve in number. The twelve Gods having charge of the living life upon the earth, drew all of their great activity power from the celestial heavens called galaxies. That power is transformed into elements, which sustain this earth in all its activities, its life, its formation, and its existence.

Their power could change those elements into forces. Through it all, and beyond human understanding, the stars in your galaxy are constantly sending that which creates elements and brings them down into the earth. This makes you what you are, has made those in the past what they were, and gives the possibility for all those in the future to be what they will be. There is not one thing going on upon earth or among the people on earth, that is not under some portion of the celestial existence of life.

God's angels have charge over each of you, so that you may draw first from the source of life. Even in your terrestrial form, you draw from this great celestial form. Eventually those of you who can rise higher in evolution and pattern, are capable of moving somewhere else which will be just as important to you as your solid ground of earth. It is important to you to make this change and advance into that greater life, so you may eventually know the Celestial Kingdom of the galaxies.

Many on earth today are in bodies foreign to their pattern. There are many that came into this earth life from places as high as the Celestial Kingdom, but have forgotten where they came from. They cannot, even for one minute, remember that they walked and talked with the Gods. They have forgotten that they were an Elohim, or that they have lived many different types of lives during the time of their evolution, or changed from one pattern to another.

The angels are never weary of taking care of their charge, nor does any Soul become weary of those in their charge, because they are ever at your service, day and night. Through your dark hours and through your light days, through your trials and tribulations, they know what is of value to you. They patiently wait until you can see clearly and act properly by the guidance of those in charge of you.

There are many, many Gods in the galaxies that have nothing to do with the human life, or any kind of life on earth. They have their work to do, if you choose to call it work. They keep this planet in space and in the center of your universe. You cannot perceive or conceive what great power it takes to keep this earth in space.

Many seekers on your earth today are wondering where they may have come from in the far distant galaxies of stars. It does not benefit students to worry about what star they came from. It is where they are today that counts, and what their intentions are for their goal of the future. Some have descended down from the Elohim body, which was created by the Father-Mother God, that oversees your pattern. Some then took on the body that you call the mortal being body, and became a fixed condition in the earth vibration. When you fulfill your earth pattern, you will know all that is necessary to continue higher. Amen. Amen. Amen.

12 Kingdoms

Gods or Powers	12	Creators
Lord Gods	12	Each Lord uses one of the Powers to create 12 elements (12 x 12 = 144)
Lords	Many	The Laws of everything
Archangels	12	Pattern Builders
Heavenly Fathers	Many	Natural Laws
Fathers	Many	Nature Laws
Elohim	Many	Sons of God; first creation of soul life
Angels	9 divisions	Service
Mortal Humans	7 divisions	2 Types: Mind and instinct
Animals	7 planes	Instincts; lower nature
Vegetables	7 divisions	Trees, plants, herbs and grasses
Minerals	7 planes	Soil, rock and water

15

HONOR ALL RACES

"From the Radiant Temple on Mt. Shasta comes the voice of experience. I give to you the greeting of the Great White Brotherhood. My Soul greets thee, my heart is filled with love for all fellow beings. I shall speak words of Truth, I shall give God praise, He is on high. Amen. Amen. Amen."

Our council has always been on the alert, not only for the changes that will take place on this earth, but the changes that take place in your vicinity, district, occupation, and in your learning experience. The greatest teacher that has ever worked upon earth is your own self, visible and invisible.

At the time the Savior was making preparations to come to the earth, the angels began their preparation 380 years before he came. They brought several advanced Master Souls to this earth to prepare the way so the Son, Elohim, could be born on earth in a virgin way. This did not mean by a female virgin, but in the sense that He had no previous karma to erase. His evolution as a generation was completed. He was giving this flesh life that He took on, to awaken the intelligence of man upon earth. Also, 380 years before your time in America, the angels began descending to this earth and preparing the way for the birth of the Israel in America. This includes the United States and

Canada.

In this century and the previous one, there have been many who have lost their lives while attempting the revelation of Truth, and for their expression of good to be the uplifting cause of humanity. Many have lost their lives in persecution, death, burning at the stake, or unknown cruelties. Man who initiates these cruelties upon his fellowman will lose his state of reason because the guilt separates him from his God Mind. The guilt has separated him from the Christ, because his humanity has ebbed away and the program of justice has been passed by.

There are those in the southern states who have been unjustly treated, those of the colored race who were intelligent, and who were bringing about their upliftment in a noble way of understanding. Some have lost their lives, even the children, because their skin was black. God does not see man's skin color except as a race pattern, but He sees the blackness in man's heart, regardless of his color. This blackness is written in the ether which can never be erased. Let this be a warning in your thinking, for such cruel acts men lose their life's pattern, regardless of how many lives they have lived in a generation.

Those of you who think religion can be set aside, and the law of God made meaningless in your country's government, or in your homes, have much to learn. You may believe in one type of religion or have faith that leads you to righteous purpose, or uphold equality of all human beings, as long as God is there, your life pattern will be the same. Regardless of your root race, it will make no difference. Here let me say that every root race has its own evolution. Although each is separate and apart from the others, there is salvation for all who live upon the earth. If anyone destroys their generation or their possibility of advancement, then many thousands of years may take place before they are capable of being born on earth again.

I would like to call to your attention one of the most important parts of the unforgivable sin; the denial of God, and refusal to allow anyone else the right to worship God in whatever way they understand. When you deny God in action, no matter where it is, you have closed the door to your God or your God understanding. When a man with intelligent training refuses to live out the pattern on earth that he recognized and took to live, that pattern is null. It is erased as if it had never been, regardless of how many lives he has lived. Man must accept and live his pattern and allow others to live their pattern.

I have shown you two different types of the denial of God in the expression of His plan. There are others. Now what transpires when a person like this dies of the physical body? There is no other pattern for him and he wanders or roams a separate space close to this earth that is not in spiritland. He goes into a region of wilderness. There is no one to talk to, no one to see, and he cannot find out who he is or where he is, until there is a mellowness or a correction within him. Only when he recognizes there is a Higher Power can his previous Guardian Angel come. Then he will be taken to one of the planets between the outer heavens and earth, not the planets that are between the sun and earth. There he passes through the experience of learning about what is good and what is not good, according to the laws of God Mind. He passes through seven rings you may call training. When he reaches the outer ring, the Guardian Angel once again meets him and brings him back through the galaxy called the Milky Way to the earth. Until then he can never return to the earth.

There was a great writer at one time who portrayed all of this training on another planet he called Hell, the planet of purification. This article was written by the man known as Dante. It is a mystical story but it does portray the Truth. Many who leave the earth after separation from their pattern have passed through the purification. When they accept the new pattern, they may find themselves in far distant jungles where the wilderness is the master of man. They must start at the very beginning of a new generation to evolve from their ignorant ways of life, by beginning with nothing. Here they work until they reach the intelligent place where life becomes illuminated to the Christness. This goes on regardless of what root race they belong to.

There are so many ways to approach the intelligence of man with Truth. Yet man, in his efforts to seek Truth, desires it to conform to the way he believes it should be. In all of the ways of teaching and preaching man's evolution, there is a golden thread of Truth. But there are so many threads in the web of destiny that they destroy the greatness of the golden thread.

In man's physical body, we teach you that the Israel are the human beings in every race that have a divided brain capacity. They have a brain that fits the visible and invisible physical life pattern, and a brain that fits the working of the God Mind in man. Until man can realize and accept the use of both the God Mind and the physical mind, how is he ever going to find the at-one-ment? Does he think there will be a bridge that he will be able to cross over without any explanation? Or will he return to the Bible's word and say, "Until the four walls or partitions are broken down and made as one, no man can enter into the kingdom of heaven."

Where are the walls? Are they in this physical body? Is it the four systems you use in this earth existence? If that is the case, there are many people breaking down their systems by their ignorant ways of living. Their physical life is destroyed before they learn more than one or two lessons. They do not allow destiny the opportunity to evolve their higher mind to rule over their lower thinking mind.

Those who expect to teach the Truth need to take into consideration that God places great value on the flesh body and the invisible body. He created these bodies so that you may have the opportunity to work out your destiny, or your plan of evolution. Man will live more or less as his neighbor is living unless he is willing to advance in his evolution. If he criticizes and condemns another root race, it is quite possible that he will have to embody in that race for a number of generations, until he purifies his thinking with equality, justness, righteousness, and mercy.

If you believe you are capable of knowing both goodness and badness, then you must live to express it. You may be asked by God, in His law of work, to serve in that purpose, so that you may teach others who have not found the answer. You cannot hide nor exclude yourself from the task of helping others and expect to advance in goodness.

When you pass on to the other side you will have the same type of service that you did here. There are many souls on the other side that belong to the lower spheres of spiritland. If you do not raise your thinking and actions above those lower spheres, you will find yourself among them. Let us stop to make a comparison here. If a man has learned a trade as a carpenter, when he dies you would not say he was an artist, pianist, architect, or any form of training he had not accomplished in his life. He will find likewise when he passes through the stage of death, he will receive his classification according to the work he was capable of doing on this side of life.

There are many who say they seek or teach Truth and light, but when they go to the other side, find they are not the teachers but they must be taught. Who teaches in these stages of spheres or planes of thinking? The Angels whom God has given charge over the earth are the teachers. Those who have been given charge of these regions, spheres, and planes, do not make mistakes for they read the pattern that God has so carefully made for the advancement of His children.

Those who are always looking out into space away from the earth, endeavor to believe they are chosen ones. They believe those in space are elected by God to give to them the first information, or the first opportunities to know the Truth. Yet each one can only accept that which he is capable of understanding. Until he is willing to be led and to believe that which he does not understand, so his capacity of wisdom expands, he cannot take it in and benefit by it.

Children of earth, every problem you have is the door to wisdom. It is the door to your freedom. Those in space who are bringing about the evolutionary changes of your earth are sent by God's administration to find those who will not waste their time in idle thinking or in secret ways of serving Truth to a select few. They seek those who will open their hearts, doors, and homes to all those who desire to partake of Truth in their own capacity of understanding, not the way that you believe they should partake of it. When you have formed opinions and made decisions without good reasoning, you only harm yourself. You are an inconvenience to others, but you cannot mar their life pattern.

Children of earth, it is not enough to say "Peace, I believe", you must do something about it. You must not believe that you are always right and that everyone else is wrong. Do not endeavor to change other people's opinions until you have changed your own. Do not believe that God cannot get along without you, for God can fill your position, your life plan at any time. Everything is written, in the symbols of the Kingdom of

Heaven, not in your words as language. Here the angels carry the words back to the thrones of the Gods, where all preparation is made long before it ever comes to earth. Evolution is a deep and wise study. It is the door to freedom where man overcomes the little ignorant self or his ego. It is where space is not limited to the weight of his physical body, but his mind can soar into the realms of Truth and the kingdoms around earth.

The council of Elder Brothers are wise and desire to share their wisdom. They know what is going on among the peoples of the earth, and about the changes on earth. They know about the changes in your government and other governments. Although freedom is spoken about as far as races are concerned, they know there will be four race divisions of this earth: the black, brown, yellow and white. When each race understands their evolution is not in their change of color, but the salvation of their pattern of life, then only will there be peace on earth. Then agreement will come among the peoples of earth and they will be like brothers and sisters living as children of God.

You who are the Israel, who have the separate division of your Divine and your physical lives on earth, should never forget every hour of your day and night to be in a constant prayer of gratitude and praise to the God you refer to as Jehovah. Let not any other man ever take you away from the principles of Jehovah. Let no other man ever tell you that God has a favorite race. Until you know the meaning of the word "race", smile when others talk. Listen to their words and give thanks in your heart that God reaches into your mind and gives to you the opportunity to think on the Thoughts of perfection. Be thankful God gives you the opportunity to know the Higher Self and allows you to pattern yourself after your Divine Being.

It is not the purpose of the Masters who return to

earth as teachers, to keep man in ignorance of what is happening on earth, how they return to the earth, or why. The Master Kingdom has made it known they are sending Master Beings to earth everywhere. This time they will not take on earth-born physical bodies to teach and uplift you as they did before Atlantis went down.

When I say Atlantis went down, I mean it disappeared under the water for purification. This land needs purification. We will hope to save this land of America so the change does not have to be under the water but can be in the air space around your earth. All beings who have evolved to the state of purification or the Christ likeness, shall not need to take on a flesh body again. They shall live in a division of space where they are quite capable of demonstrating their worth.

Before I close, the question has come to a student's mind about what you can do to help those who have passed over into spiritland. One of the many needs of those in spiritland is the realization that they have passed through death, and may not be required to come back to earth if they will make their progression on the other side in spiritland. As you have schools for educational development on earth, so likewise in spiritland there are schools even for the children who did not live long on earth.

Now you must realize that if a Soul has taken a new pattern and the opportunity of being reborn on earth, they take on the seven steps of life, as well as the seven steps of death. The manifestation or destiny they have taken on are the seven deadly sins. If they do not live long when they come on earth, they will still be held in that infant pattern, and they must begin life training as the infant on the invisible side of the physical life in spiritland. Schools there are quite capable of giving them the advantage of every part of the lives they have lived in a generation, as this information is sealed or recorded in their book of life.

Youth who come to the invisible side of life find great schools known as the schools of knowledge. There they are taught by wise ones who give them the training of what they may expect if they return to earth. These teachers also demonstrate, by taking them to many places on earth where they can see the manifestations of effort, and the effects that are caused by life.

There are many adults who have lived close to their allotted time. This means as they have lived enough time to exemplify the infant, youth, and adult, as well as the mental training, Soul training and the spiritual training within the number of years they lived on earth. These are the divisions on the invisible side of life also, but there is a space between your visible physical existence called life and the invisibility of spiritland.

It takes seventy-two hours to cross the divide from one side to the other and this is referred to as crossing the River Jordan. River means the conscious awakening and Jordan means darkness. So when those who pass into this River Jordan of darkness with no capacity or training of Truth, the training must take place. This work is done by those who are left on earth that can contact them, and those on the invisible side known as their Guardian Angels.

Those who go out quickly by accident or those in the service of their country who give their life, are in the capable hands of the angels who have been given charge over them. Let us say that if evolution can be recognized by incarnation and reincarnation, it is quite possible that thousands or even millions that were on the other side, have agreed after their training to come back on earth and take on a life, and to give it for freedom of others in their experiences or destiny of life. In giving that life, many times they have earned their freedom. Amen. Amen. Amen.

16

ILLUMINATION

"My Soul greets thee. My heart is filled with Love for all fellowmen. I shall speak words of Truth by these lips and I give praise to God on High. Let us all praise God on High. Amen. Amen. Amen."

To give praise to God on High is to praise the work of the Higher Self. The Higher Self is the only God you can know. The councilors can recognize a higher work of God, while you in mortal flesh, can only recognize the Higher Self within you, as the Law that is written in the ethers. When you hear us say the words, "Amen, Amen, Amen", we are acknowledging the closing of the Law to the three divinities within every man.

Perhaps when you look at those who study spiritual qualities, you may wonder why there are not more illuminated ones. This is a day and age when you believe man is intelligent and capable of understanding. The answer is quite simple. There are too many attractions that distract you from the constant effort of the manifestation of Christness. Perhaps for one hour of each day your thoughts are indeed sincere and true, and you make every effort to continue on in the highest fold. Yet another hour goes by and something tears you down, tries and tempts you, and you have to overcome it all before you can realize illumination.

If you should see a man, who suddenly became

illuminated, he would walk as a stranger among his friends of the past. They would say he was not right, and might try to confine him. He could not partake of today's life and only be illuminated for just part of the time; it cannot be done. That is why the Masters are making such a great effort at this time before the coming change. We desire to help the beings of your earth and in space, to meet the conditions that will exist. There will be many illuminated ones to come through, so you will not walk alone nor be a stranger among those not yet illuminated.

We watch students who believe they can put what they find as spiritual Truth into words to teach other people. However, illumination is not something you can put in words for any student not yet awakened to understand. As Yessue Ben Miriam taught His disciples, He first began to teach them in parables, as you have read them in the Bible. They did not understand until they progressed mentally to the level where illumination did not separate the Higher Self from the lower self. I am speaking of the Mind when I say Christness, the Spiritual Sense. Physical senses cannot grasp the deep meaning, for Christness is illumination. If any of you are illuminated, how can you explain it to others?

It is indeed a problem among people on the earth to understand the difference between Spiritland and Masterland. It is a simple problem to understand. As long as you have a mental concept of a physical form that needs to be created, you will continue to come back to earth. In spiritland you eventually realize that you do have to return to earth.

In the Masterland you do not create a physical body that lives and dies, goes to spiritland and begins anew. You work entirely in the Soul form, and are not connected with mental and physical bondage. In God

Mind everything is natural in conception and creation; there is no mystery or selfishness in the creation of your own Soul pattern.

When you create a physical form, and come from spiritland, your Guardian Angel must take you to a place to be reborn on earth that will accept your pattern. Once you take on that conception to be born through parents into a new form, you may not like what you have accepted. Perhaps you will be a dwarf and you will not like it. That is what you have chosen and you must work out your pattern through it. Perhaps you may have chosen to be a giant alongside of your brothers, sisters, and parents, and you will feel that you are out of place in this world because your form does not fit with others. You have chosen it! Until you are willing to accept, and abide by the opportunity to work out your pattern, you come again and again.

If you seek beauty but you have not earned beauty, you will not have it. If beauty was your weakness before, then you do not have it. If you have worked out the problems that have torn apart your heart and mind, if you have overcome them without selfishness, or any animosity toward your parents or your problems, then you may find a beautiful form to show you that you have made a perfection, perhaps not in mind but in body. One of the greatest measures of reason is, that a beautiful form does not have a good mind. Usually those that are beautiful are shallow because they have fulfilled one of their life's patterns and desires, but have forgotten the greater portion that goes with it.

I encourage each one of you to smile more, speak more kindly and do little deeds of goodness for others. Try not to remember your good deeds, but do them because you love to serve. This will not make a beautiful face for you, yet, when you are able to glance into the fourth dimension and see your Higher Self, you would fall down on your knees at the beauty which you cannot see in yourself now. It is also good to take into consideration a moderation of voice, learn to speak kindly and not defensively. If unpleasant things are said, do not answer back. Within yourself you can think, "God understands", and that Higher Self of you is God. All that matters in your world is that you do the best you can, shirking nothing because it seems laborious. Do your work as you would do it for God, and nothing will hinder you in finding illumination.

Little things that you pass by are the stepping stones on the path of illumination. We councilors in the Temple consider deeply that you are not hiding away from the world, you are living in it, while those in far away places hide in mountains, caves, and away from the world to become the adept. They have no way to reach out and give to the world, because they have the thought of gaining for self alone. I do not cast any reflection on those of the selfless type, but I do find for illumination you cannot shut yourself away from the world. You are in the world and you are here to work. "Pick up your bed and walk", as Jesus said, because as long as you lie in a helpless condition you are bound to come back again to work out the problems you laid aside.

I wish to speak about age. There are some of you of tender years that find you are old. You have learned too quickly the useless things but you are learning too slowly the spiritual things. We see those of you who are older not according to your age, but we see the work you are doing for others as you would do for God. Age on your side of life is numbered by the years that the sun has come and gone. On this side we measure what you have done, and how you have gained by your efforts. So we see you as a pattern, not as a person, but that does not mean that we are not as close to you as your breath, even if you do not see us in form or hear us speak.

You must submit all of your mortal life expression to your Soul's correction. You must have divine love in you heart for all your fellowmen; not to pamper, not to give without understanding, but to be able to help your fellowmen to stand upon their own feet, which is the Law. The words of Truth in the Temple were written long before man on earth can conceive. The council cannot change those words or Laws: they are written Laws. Only elements committed to the written Laws can be used on earth. Many mistakes are made because of man's interference with that law.

I would like to talk with you a little about what Mastership means. When you speak to others about the Masters, often they will look at you and wonder if you are intelligent. Keep in mind that in every part of teaching intelligent work, whether it is school work, missionary work, religious work, art, or culture, there are different approaches to reach a better understanding.

Your Catholic religion and many other religions, teach you of the saints. You read and hear the philosophy written in scripts and theories. They tell you this one was a saint, and another was an angel. Protestant religions talk about the Christ and the Christness. All of them explain that to become any of these, you must have overcome death.

Now overcoming death means when you die, you do not come back in a flesh body again. If you have discarded all need for your shadow body and your flesh body, you have no need of spiritland. So when you overcome death, you go to some other place, but they fail to tell you where this other place is. They call it heaven and they point up in the sky. They cannot prove the existence of heaven, yet they say they can prove the fourth dimension. They teach in school as an educational principle that there is a fourth dimension, the one above the third dimension.

You live in the third dimension in this flesh body, and spiritland is in the invisible side of the third dimension. When you enter into the fourth dimension, it is some other place that you do not see or know about, but may have heard about. No one tells you if it is above you, beyond your head, right with you as you stand upon earth, or if it is in the ground. Few dare to teach about it, because they cannot prove it. Your Bible calls it, "That place in Heaven". There are three heavens and it does not state which one of those heavens it is.

In some religions they teach some people become saints who have passed through death, laid in the tomb, and have been prayed out of it. If you are prayed out of your tomb, where have you been while in the tomb? They do not answer those questions, but they lead you to believe two different methods. In the Catholic religion, a priest or his family must pay out so much, even if he is a Cardinal or a Pope, before he can become a saint. That is false. If you are a saint or a master, you are already one as you ascend when you die to the flesh. It takes seventy-two hours to disconnect the cord that is called the silver cord that binds the two bodies together on earth. Once those bodies are loosened and your book of life is closed, then you can ascend or go to where you belong.

Jesus was laid in a tomb so it was said. On the third day, after seventy-two hours, they went to bury Him and He was not there. That is a story, but it does demonstrate the Truth. You may be in your tomb, this physical body, when you die, and the third day you will ascend, whether it is to spiritland, or above the mortal earth world of man, to a higher dimension.

Those that we call Masters are the Ascended Ones, whether they are called Saints, Angels, or Christ: they are the Ascended Ones. When they ascend, according to what their life pattern was to work out on earth, they go into the realm where they can do their greatest work to assist the fulfillment of the Christness in man still upon earth. When they say St. Germain, St. Peter, St. Luke, St. Gabriel and St. John, they are simply saying they are Ascended Ones. They are Masters in our words.

When I first came to earth to teach, I descended into a flesh body and was known as a high priest. That was as good as saying I was like a God. At that time they did not know Jesus, the Christ, of two thousand years ago. But, I found I could not live the life of a saint, so I misused the Holy Fire, and I became enmeshed in the flesh of earth. I helped create the flesh of the earth before I became a wanderer upon the face of the earth. After misusing the Holy Fire I spent my time seeking more Light and understanding of how to go back to that kingdom from which I had strayed.

In Christianity, they teach you about the Son of God. They are trying to make you believe there was just one son, which could never be you, but you could be like Him. All the God you will ever know when you are in a flesh body, is the Son of God in you as the Christness, and you CAN be like Him. How could you believe there is a God that would only give something that you could look upon and idolize or worship? Well, that is exactly what the religions do when they say the Christ died upon the cross to save you. You are the Christ and you crucify Him every day. You are in the Jesus body, and you are the only one that can crucify the Christ in you, the Son of God.

Many of you think and talk about God as if He were sitting somewhere in the sky above you. Some say he sits with a rod to hit you on the head, pass, or wave over you, so that you will be different, and be treated differently from others of your mortal friends and families. How silly to believe that God has all power to create the heavens and earth, and all things in, on, and above; yet be such a one sided thing to think about. Religion as taught is often stupidity. Living is life, and the spirit of God is in every man equally, but every man does not use it equally.

In man's spiritual education he begins to know himself, find his freedom, see without the mote in the eye, and hear without the sting. He learns to do and give, without telling God how to do or give. To give in God's name means you have relinquished all claim. To give for the betterment of your fellowman is only stepping aside and letting God use what is His own. Nobody can own this planet. The Gods who created this planet are watching over it, and there are many Gods watching this earth. The God that we are talking about is in you, and is the God that created the mortal being of you. It gives you the opportunity to return back to that Sainthood.

There is no need to ponder, "Should I or should I not ask God to do this or that"? All you have to do is give thanks that you have recognized a need, knowing the answer has been already fulfilled. How would you ever know lack if you did not know there had once been abundance? You are like this instrument, when we began to teach her to let go of those mighty binding cords of earth that creep into your habits and thinking world. She began to realize that her home life was a part of it; she believed to get along in this world meant saving in many ways. When she peeled a potato, you could read a newspaper through the peeling. It was a difficult task to impress upon her, that she was not allowing God's abundance to express.

That is the way many of you are. Do not be afraid of using what God gives you to use. There is much more than you will ever be able to use up in your life, if you will use it correctly. The reason you see scarcity is because you do not know how to use abundance. Is it a crime for a man to own money? It is a crime to own money if you do not know how to use it. When you use it selfishly, or always saving because you believe God cannot take care of you, then you are misusing it. You need to remove from your own thinking mind that there is a shortage, and that you must burden yourselves with many troubles just to hang onto a little bit of your money. You must remember that you can lose your money as you sleep.

The Councilors and I pray for each one of you. When we say pray, we give praise that each of you are growing mentally and physically. We pray that you are meeting your trials, your temptations and your troubles, not with fear and anguish, but with a desire of doing something about them. If you desire to help someone overcome conditions that seem to bind them, go about it with praise in your heart that God takes care of His own. Then let Him do it. For the moment you see that God is not working, then the God in you cannot work either.

In teaching the work, we must break down the binding habits and bring to each one of you the Presence of God in you, so you can realize it. Then you are able to recognize where to make the changes. You cannot pray to God to make changes: you must make them yourself. I give you the blessings of the Radiant Temple and all who are at the Council Table give you their blessings. We hope that each one of you shall renew faith in yourself, and know there is work for you to do, and that you are going to do it. Amen. Amen. Amen.

17

CHANGE YOUR MIND, CHANGE YOUR LIFE

"I give to you the greetings of the Great White Brotherhood. My Soul greets thee. My heart is filled with Love for all fellowmen. I shall speak words of Truth, giving praise to God on High. Amen. Amen. Amen."

When man can see his life, as small as the little creeping ant on the earth, then he can see how all men are created equal. That equality is not just color or race, it is the interior personality. I suggest, if you want to take your rightful place in the future, do not go downward, go upward. Never debate with anyone or lower your good qualities, but seek everyday to improve your higher qualities. Some people on the earth today believe they are covering up their true appearance by their paint and make-up, but they are only playing with deception. It will grow into their character and will live with them all of the rest of the generation. I offer this to you who seek to be spiritual, because it is the Truth.

I watch many students play the part of affection. They say words that are not real and they call others "sisters" and "brothers", but that is not the correct interpretation. Rather it should be that all men have a place of work. It is work to live what you came to overcome and respect all others that you contact. Even though someone may smite you on the cheek or belittle you, when you can see them in the true light, you see they are working out a pattern. In these things you begin to understand the light, and know what brotherhood and sincerity mean.

Spiritual quality avoids notice of the difference of bodies, and shows you a man's mind must fit a body to be on certain levels. Until you can purify your body to make it equal to your intention, and perfect your Spiritual Self to the level of your Soul, you cannot say you know brotherhood or brotherly love. When anyone shows the resistant disposition, or shows opposition, then he is not on the path of light. Regardless of where he is, if he does not accept his own pattern, he becomes a wanderer on earth. If he will not learn in this life, he is certainly doomed to come back and relive the life. Giving up is so easy, yet all man has to do is change. Man of your day would rather be stubborn and resist change, determined that he knows best, rather than submit to his Higher Self.

From the Temple, we see those who go through ceremonies and certain motions of their bodies. They say certain words or sounds and do it all in the name of spiritual Truth, believing that their Spirit is doing this. While the Spirit looks on, I cannot say it weeps, but it can be that it grieves, for your Higher Self knows everything about you. It knows when you are sincere and where your weaknesses are, and it loves you in the love of the Christness. Though you may take a long time, you will enter the fold, and your Higher Self will never complain.

It is quite possible that your Higher Self can communicate with you by sound. It is quite possible if you dream and you believe your dreams have meaning, that your Higher Self can talk with you through your dreams. Are you willing to listen? Are you unafraid to hear? Do you desire that communication more than anything else in life? When you receive Truth, are you willing to share it? These are the questions you must ask yourself.

Many ask, "How am I ever going to learn, how do I know"? I will tell you. The moment you ask for Truth and refuse to be satisfied with anything else, you are on the road of learning, but it is not an easy path. You become the neophyte, willing to acknowledge when you are right and willing to acknowledge when you are wrong.

In listening to many conversations among people, this one believes they are right, the other believes they are right, and how are you going to settle it? There is but one way. When the Master, Yessue Ben Miriam, came to earth to teach mortal man how he could understand the working of his Higher Self, He taught man awareness of wickedness by showing him that he had a conscience. Each one of you have a conscience. It has been trained quite a number of times in your lives on earth. Your conscience tells you when you are right and when you are wrong. If you do wrong against your conscience, knowing all the while what is right, then you have committed a sin, an error, and what many call karma.

Each time you commit or repeat that error, you must learn over again. What you have already learned in yourself about what is good and what is wrong, you do not have to repeat. When you experience sadness, regret, and are deeply moved, then your conscience is telling you that you are wrong. When something takes place, passes by, and leaves only pleasant memories, you know you have been right and you do not have to repeat the lesson again. Those of you who have joined your lives together may find regrets, or some little part unfinished, then you must come back and complete it.

This is the law; it is the principle which you must work out. No one else can do this for you.

Those things that you find at the end of the day, year, or end of time, that make you sad, that you have not paid enough attention to or regret, produce remorse. When you pass on to the other side, your Guardian Angel will show you how the book of life is balanced. That is why so many spirits in spiritland waste no time in coming back. Many feel they will not advance until they get back to earth and undo the things they committed that left them torn. Spiritland is a school for the departed, not a place to school those on earth.

There is a difference between the man with a conscience and a man who is not awakened as yet. Those who have committed great crimes, leave sorrow and troubles in their wake. They have no remorse because they have no conscience, not because they are more cruel than you. To be born without a conscience is a terrific path for any man to travel. So before you judge others, ponder how much you have to undo concerning remorse, regrets and sadness in your own life.

There is a misunderstanding that I would like to speak to you about. Much is said against the heathen tribes, but they are the only ones who are living the natural sexual life on earth. Now do not misunderstand when I say no other people on the earth are living a natural sexual life; I am not pointing my finger at any one person. You will find that in the far north, or among the bushmen, or in the pure black race, they are clean of fornication. This word has been used many times in the teachings of preachers, ministers and the wise men. They have used the word, fornication, but they seldom gave out the Truth of its meaning. They have also used the word "adultery", to make you believe that it was something wrong in sexual life.

Adultery or fornication refers to the mixing of the

blood patterns of the four different root races: black, yellow, brown and white. If a black man mixes his blood pattern with any other race he has committed adultery. If a white man has committed a mixture with another race he has committed adultery. The seed from that adultery may take thousands of years to go back to its natural seed. It is the same as your plants. If they are interfered with they might be more attractive in their form of buds and colors, but they are adulterated and are not natural. If you leave them alone they will go back to their natural state, and it is the same with all races or tribes upon this earth.

Now what is meant by fornication? It is an absolutely unnatural sex activity that destroys any one tribe by the mixture of the blood race patterns. Fornication means untruth or unnatural. Whole tribes of people have been destroyed because they mixed their blood patterns. The last of Atlantis to go down was destroyed because of mixing the blood patterns. Only the seeds passed down from Abraham were pure. So Abraham does not mean a Jew, Abraham means the father of pure seed, the father of the Israel, of which Jesus, Yessue Ben Miriam, was a descendent.

How do you accept the lessons that you are meeting daily in your mind and pattern? Lessons are the experiences you come in contact with everyday, not what is written or taught to you orally. The patterns that you contact in your daily walk of life are the things you have not accepted before, or that you have tried to avoid. If you put it off, it only delays what is most essential for you to learn. Only experience is the answer.

If you must meet poverty, accept it, because it gives you the opportunity to experience want. Want builds desire, and unless your desire is great enough, how can the answer be given? Your Masters assist by bringing answers to you, so that you have enough desire to continue seeking. Though something may wait for you a hundredfold on the outside, unless you open your mind and heart to desire, it cannot manifest. That is why we tell you before you even ask, God has supplied. The supply is there to take, but you must have enough faith to manifest it in your aura first, then in your physical existence second. If you are stubborn, you will not find the path easy. You must lay aside your stubborn nature and accept the unexplainable, until you have grown to see and know, beyond a doubt, the invisible realm.

We teach things to fill any heart with joy and happiness but we do not find the empty place to put it. Instead we find stubborn natures, fixed opinions, and decisions made without clarity. We work with these seekers here and in other places everyday.

So to begin with, as a most sincere seeker, one must desire the Truth above all other things. Self-importance does not count. Though you may tell God over and over again you desire to live a spiritual life and you want spiritual demonstration, if you live in a glass house, you must tear the house down yourself. You must rebuild the house piece by piece by your deeds. You must find and accept the answers to your questions and know it as Truth.

The pit of your being, your solar plexus, is in constant contact with your physical mind and organs. The physical ductless glands allow the function of the nature laws within your body. At the very moment you desire proof, explanations of wisdom, and obedience to the Christ law, you will find the path rugged and the mountain steep. But if your will and desire is strong enough you can overcome any part of it. You do not ask the mountain to be brought to you: you go to the mountain. There you will find that God has been generous and gives opportunity to every man on earth.

All seekers have an active faculty of intuition. The "intu" is what is most important to remember. The "in" and the "tu" are combined into motivation and motion, cause and effect. Little things on your side of life indicate the many spiritual forms, both of spiritland and of the educational realm of the Master Kingdom.

The best advice we can give to people who seclude themselves in the silence is to speak out a little more than they do. They should speak out about what needs to be done for the Truth. When a student expresses a desire to know Truth, it does not always mean that the door is open. Unless the door is open, he cannot possibly see the philosophy of the Soul.

Those of you who feel you are ready for higher things have often held back things you don't understand or cannot accept. The truth is, in the end all seekers are the same. You may work wholeheartedly morning, noon, and night, but there are things you avoid or set aside. You never make time to fathom their depth of Truth or work them out, so things are passed by which may hold the key to your Higher Self.

Those on the invisible side of life from spiritland or the higher space, return to this earth and endeavor to lead or encourage those that work to improve their patterns. We have no objections to those that return from spiritland as long as they give Truth. If they understood Truth before they left the earth they will not forget it, for you do not forget anything that lifts you high spiritually. You also remember those things that kept you low, for they contain the pattern you must follow and work out. Man, in the physical body, goes along in his own pattern as he pleases and as it seems to fit him. He is sometimes grateful for words of encouragement, but he seldom gives up his own opinions.

The Masters who come have a Spiritual Body not a

flesh body. It is not a spirit body. We have a Spiritualized body that has no density to it whatsoever, unless we desire to manifest it in form on earth. If we manifested in form on your streets, in public places, or even in your homes, you would be frightened. We understand the nature of the human beings and their fears, we see it everyday. So we do not manifest anything that will cause fear among you.

If you went to bed at night intending to sleep, and you saw vision after vision, face after face, do you think you would not be frightened? Perhaps some visions may be pleasant but not all, because you would not understand them. Therefore we do not push students into psychic visions they do not understand. There are those quite capable who do hear from the higher realms. Because some of you do not hear, understand, or recognize different sounds, you think it is something mysterious. When your intelligence moves into the fourth dimension for a fraction of time, and you hear as your Higher Self, you find it mysterious. That is why it is necessary to intelligently train the students to be able to function in their physical bodies and yet also function in their invisible physical body.

When you see visions, they are not within you, but in the space around you. It is not the same space in which you breath or live in your physical body. It is the space you go to when you sleep, your dream state. The body that you dream in is your mental body and when it is freed of this physical weight, it can move out into space. In this space, away from the flesh, you can hear, see, learn, or go through experiences. It seems like a dream when you come back, but each dream is symbolic, because there is no language except symbols on the other side. Your mental mind thinks it must be a dream because you do not have the language of the symbols, so you compare what you received in your dream to how you live upon earth.

There are many seekers who want the highest, but it takes patience, steadfastness, loyalty, attention, love, faith and fellowship. If you only listen but do not work out your problems, you will never know the Truth. Even though you say, "I like it, I believe it, I think it is good, I think it is a right way", if you do not know truth for yourself, you cannot answer others truthfully. There are those with stubborn natures who listen to Truth, but only believe in their way. They explore the rules and regulations of how the world is run and the creation of their physical bodies, but cannot accept anything that is opposite to their set opinion.

Not one man or woman can create the seed of life. The spark that you call passion, only opens the door for life on earth. The seed of life is what God has created, and no man can do likewise. Many times we have heard parents say, "This is MY child". How little do they know. The only part that belongs to the parents is the opportunity to serve that life. The child belongs to God. Most parents will admit that God gave the child life, and God can take the life when He sees fit.

You know there are some leaders governing your nations and countries doing their best, and accomplishing more for the people than previous leaders have done. Against the odds they work out the problems of security for the people on earth. There are always those who sit around and watch, who think they could figure out a program, or work out a better plan. If that was so, God would have put them in the high place. Whether you believe it or not, God chooses the ones in high places to work out the problems, plans, and the life patterns of those upon the earth. Whether it is your race or another, that race will work out its progressive plan, regardless of what you think will work.

If all the people upon the earth are destroyed, which

you will admit is possible, you would not stop God's progression. If you do not progress in this world, you are going to have to progress in the next world. On earth you can progress of your own free will, but when you go into the other kingdoms, you do not have free will. You progress because that is the law. Do you believe the laws that govern life can be as fickle as the laws that you break on earth? You claim, "I did not intend to do it. I did not feel I was doing something wrong." You believe the laws are made for the other man, not for yourself, but that is not the way it is when you go to the other side.

There is one true way, and the only hell you will know is when you refuse to progress. If hell was a place of dire punishment so severe that God would have nothing to do with it, what are the punishments of those that live on earth and suffer? Why would God let them suffer? The answer is, hell is on this side, except when you will not progress on the other side. There is no burning furnace, no shoveling of coal and no devil that will prod you: you prod yourself.

Now where did the theme of the devil come from? It comes from the lower races of man, some that are within the earth, some live upon the earth, and some that live in space. Until you understand them I would not advise you to form fantastic ideas or pictures in your state of consciousness that you cannot erase. Seek to find and understand that which is true. Then you become a Christ-like person, not because you belong to any order or creed, but because you endeavor to live true to the Christ Consciousness within you. When you do that, you have all of the religion that man can absorb on this earth.

It is quite natural to understand that far back in your history there have been good people and evil people. Those that are evil you say have gone to hell.

How will you ever know? Those that you say are good, you believe have gone to heaven. How will you ever know, unless you take the opportunity to understand the meaning of hell and heaven. Very few religions teach you the Truth about heaven and hell.

The position of a teacher makes him no greater than the student. The position of the head of any religion makes them no greater than the follower. Jesus said, "Why callest thou Me good, for none are good." This was the greatest Master that ever appeared on earth to teach man salvation. He did not say, "I will die on the cross to save you. I shall bleed to death to save you." That is not true. He taught that when you take on the cross, the physical body, it becomes your chance to find everlasting life. It is your opportunity to find the Christness within you. Amen. Amen. Amen.

18

ANSWERS TO QUESTIONS

Often at the end of a discourse, the Masters gave the opportunity for those present to ask questions. We have included a few of the questions asked and the answers received in this chapter.

Q. Could you please advise me on how to be of the greatest service to God and to my fellowman? I am concerned about the welfare of other people, and I want to do what God wants me to do with all my heart.

A. There is a great change coming upon the earth. We cannot tell you the exact day or hour, nor where it will come first. Always there must be those at the head of God's missionary work, to save lives, feed the hungry and clothe those in need. If you give your wealth it makes no difference, it is you that God asks for in service. In your Bible, it says, "The harvest is abundant but the harvesters are few." Truly the harvest is almost ready, but the prepared harvesters are few.

There is much to learn about the Truth of God and man's misunderstanding of it. Man goes through many useless things in the false belief that he is walking in the steps of light as the Son of God did. Often he is absolutely standing in his own light. To many the worship of God is like worshipping an idol, but joy in the heart is not idol worship. Joy in the heart is your reflection of the Christ life. Let joy be in your heart and words of kindness come forth from your lips, and you will never regret that you stand in the presence of God who is always with you.

We know your desire is to serve, and that is good, but first it must be taken apart for deeper understanding. The goodness given to other people must first be served to self. If you do not have goodness in you, how can you understand what goodness is, so you can serve others? First you must understand and live Truth, so when you give that Truth, others feel it, absorb it, and then are capable of living it. You cannot generously give wealth to others and expect them to become Christ-like. You can show them by helping to teach them the Truth, but let them live their own life pattern.

My Elder Brother, Yessue Ben Miriam, often says, not to pray telling God what to do, but listen as you pray for what God tells you to do. While you pray telling God to do for others, you are believing in a power that is greater than what God wants man to use. You are then commanding. God does not command you, why then should you command God?

Pray believing that the God Power is all over the earth. Pray believing all men can awaken and take from the space about them, what God has for them, and what they have earned in their previous lives. If they will not learn except by stumbling, falling, and going through miseries of sickness or sorrows, let them have their fill of it. Accept with blessings that God has you to help them. Pick them up when they are ready, and encourage them to overcome their sickness and sorrows. Let them see life's lesson can be their greatest joy, and that they have the opportunity to work it out for full understanding. In this way, you find yourself entwined to the power of God, and that is service.

Those who offered to serve Jesus on earth, did not want to give up their old ways of life. They wanted to serve, but they tried to make a bargain. God does not accept bargains. Jesus said, "Go into the different parts of the world, the four corners, and preach the Truth." What does preaching mean? It does not mean that you should stand on a box or someplace high over people, and shout about condemnation of hell or heaven. Preaching means to speak Truth, share it, and be ever ready to serve it. Never condemn anyone in the name of religion, for no man knows the pattern of another. If God chooses a man to take out all the brutish nature of his life, let it be. God knows the limit of all men and their patterns, and He will take care.

You can bless others, pray that their Masters may work with them and direct them into the Truth, the same as you have been directed and guided. When man comes to earth with his pattern, he is not told he has but one path to go. He is shown that he can choose his path, and determine how he will follow it. If he chooses the rough path, it will be the shortest way to Truth. If he chooses the long rosy path, with no temptations or trials, and all things come easily, he will not understand God is not choosing him above his fellow man.

The man who is willing to face all his problems, meeting those problems in the highest purity, finds that is the cleansing. When one error is washed away, he can take another problem and solve it, thus, step by step, he gains wisdom with understanding. Wisdom of itself only makes wise fools, but wisdom with understanding makes God men out of mortals.

Q. Could you please explain more about the germ of the Christness?

A. Christ is a germ that is born in the conscious state of existence in man. It is plain to see, there are many on the earth today that do not have a conscious conscience, or a consciousness that will accept the impressions of light. This is because the germ has not been born into them yet. Those who claim to be on a spiritual path try to express, that the germ of the Christ Spirit has been born into them. Jesus Christ was endeavoring to tell you that when He said, "You must be born again." The birth that is explained in your Bible is a parable, to show that the Christ was born and is in everyone. The three wise men are the three stages of consciousness that must be awakened by the birth of the Christ. Christ is a word that means perfection. The Father represents the Spirit of the Holy Breath that gives life to man, and the Mother represents the pure nature.

The Christ Man came to teach and demonstrate all the necessities for man. He chose His twelve disciples meaning the twelve faculties. First, he had to overcome the lower sense faculties through the temptations, desires of nature and the possessiveness of greed. As the Christness is born into man, the twelve faculties awaken and bring the light, but not the light of the third dimension. Until man is ready to accept this birth of the Christ germ, which is the desire for Truth, light, perfection, eternal life and the knowledge of God in himself more than anything else, he will never start on the path of light. The germ grows with the understanding of faith, hope, love, mercy, patience, and willingness.

The Bible speaks of John baptizing Jesus, the Son. The word John represents love, and Jesus represents the flesh man. The dove that descended upon Him is peace. When it said, "In whom I AM well pleased," the I AM is well pleased when man will let It take over and guide his steps. Your Bible speaks of water many times and gives countless explanations. I take you to the book of Genesis where it tells about making the waters below and the waters above. The meaning of the waters above refers to Thoughts, and the waters below to worldly thinking, for Thoughts do not come into the world of flesh. Thoughts can only be sensitized by man's thinking about their meanings.

The Bible tells you Jesus was baptized in the River Jordan. If you will look up the translation of Jordan, you will find that the River Jordan refers to crossing over into the true life, not death, but the life of light, understanding, and change, to become the man you were created to be. Water represents Thoughts that guide and direct you, reminding you that you are always guided and directed by the True Thoughts.

The fountain of living water carries the source from your higher God Self to your lower flesh self. Your flesh cannot think, but its sensations of the five senses can cause you to think. Only by the crucifixion of your thinking will this source penetrate into your subconsciousness or sleep consciousness, to awaken the germ of the Christness as the reflection of your Higher Self.

There never was any type of a Christ man that the Israel was not connected to. Christ came to save those who were lost from the fold and He went out to the mountain to find the lost sheep or the lamb that may have strayed. Understand that sheep represent physical thinking and the lamb is the Pure Thought. He went after the lamb, the Christness in you. The Christness in every man who desires Truth will find that pure Thought, which is the germ that will grow into you, and into every man's consciousness. There are many who will reject the story of the Christ on earth, because it is not what they desired or heard before. There are many who will believe Christ is coming again, and He is coming again, but He will come in each man's own life who is an Israel.

There will be Masters with this Christness born in them who will come to earth, and they are among you at this time. Until you see the Christness as I have described it, you will not be able to recognize them when you speak with them. Until man is ready to lay aside all false concepts, while not giving up the true Christness, or throwing away the God of creation, but he must prepare to expand out his greatness of mind. Man must see beyond the earth fold and recognize the reality of the true existence of his universe.

Q. If we work on our own karma, does it gradually take care of the world karma too?

A. Anything that would help one student go one step higher will naturally help people of the whole world. I could not say to what extent that the help could be noticed. If you have 20,000 people struggling to reach a higher step, something would be noticed in different environments of work, business, or education. They say that a drop of water can wear away a stone. Perhaps you would not notice it at the beginning, but the water would leave its imprint and be noticed.

If each of you could understand, the divinity of God is divided into a heavenly state and an earthly state. There are divisions within each of them that all human beings must pass through. Before you can reach Divinity, you must pass through mortality. There is nothing that man can do except alleviate some of his own karma, or just plain wrong-doing. The only way you can undo wrong is turn around and do what is right.

If you are conscientious in your thinking, sit down

and say to yourself, not to God, "Let God's will be done." You still have to listen and discern the positive and the negative. You do not, however, have to be the judge of what is right and wrong, for in your act of judgment, you may be wrong. The best act a seeker can do is sit down, and say to the Great Power in them, "Here I am, whatever Thou wilt have me do, let me do it." Then do not be concerned about what is transpiring in the world around you, for that is God's business. Too many people are telling God how to do His work. Long before they were a small germ in the great plan of mankind, the earth made its changes and alleviated or disposed of many on the earth ready to make a change.

Perhaps I have taken the long way around to tell you to be at peace. Sit down and commune with God about His great work that concerns YOU, and let the rest of the world be taken care of by God's Administering Angels. In this way you greatly advance your own plan, and become a great help to the God plan in its unfolding.

Q. Phylos, could you help us understand the problem of resentment?

A. Resentments come from lessons, and unless students are willing to work out their lessons, they will carry them over into another life. Some have carried their lessons from as far back as the Atlantian time or before, and have not rid themselves of those lessons yet. We have no limit of time here. Only you see time as it measures out your days, weeks, months and years.

Knowing students by their patterns, we see what they have to overcome. Overcoming may not be exactly the correct word to use. If you saw a fire, you might be able to overcome it, if your desire was great enough to do all you could in your way to quench it. Sometimes that is not the right way. Some people feel if they gather all their troubles, trials, tribulations and complaints, and keep them in silence, they have overcome. Problems cannot be overcome by hiding them, or hiding from them. They will still be there. They must still be taken out and overcome by dissolving them. Dissolving means understanding them, and doing something about it yourself.

Many people say all their troubles are caused by someone else. You make your own troubles, arguments, disinterest or interest in good things. Nobody else has a thing to do with it. Resentment is as wrong as jealousy, and to try to hide either one is not the way to overcome them. Get it out in the open. If you are guilty of resentment, agree with it, understand it, and do away with it. Hiding it or being silent about it, is not peaceful. There are those who feel they are peaceful because they will not help someone else understand their problem, and refuse to understand it themselves. Only dissolving does away with the problem because it helps your pattern, and the other patterns involved in it.

Avoiding Truth is never the way to the door of Truth. Truth is found wherever you look. If you find it and hide it, you do not have it in your possession, and will not be able to use it. Doing things that are useful will not excuse you from things you have hidden away. Those are the things you call secrets. You will find when you pass over to the other side, that the closet you held your secrets in, has an open door and many can see inside. Those who see will not condemn you, but will help you find your way back to earth to overcome your mistakes.

If you can see your errors, you can overcome them in this life. It is the willingness to meet your problems face to face, that does away with sin and karma. All of your experiences, good or bad, come to you from your first three Masters. They test you everyday of your life, hoping that one of those lessons will open the door to your wisdom. Once you see the light, there is never again the darkness. It is not how much you have read, or what someone else has explained that is truth to you. Your truth is found in unfolding experiences and overcoming them. That is overcoming death. Unresolved experiences will bring on death and another life pattern.

Q. Will you please tell us how the planets and stars affect us while we live on the earth?

A. There has to be a great change among the people of the earth as well as a change on the planet earth. It is going on inside and it will come to the outside of the earth. Great planetary influences are becoming stronger everyday upon the earth. Some of the planets have ruled or influenced the earth for given periods of time such as; twenty, fifty, eighty or a hundred years, and many changes take place. Without these changes and influences, there would be no advancement, progression, or evolution.

There are other planets, like the star force, approaching your universe. They are on the border of it at the present time and will cause great changes that will affect the earth. Naturally, anything strong enough to change the earth will have its effect within the cosmic ether around earth, and you are in that cosmic ether.

Some of you cannot understand why the tension is so strong for good and also for evil. It is everywhere because the elements of cosmic space are changing. There are new elements being let loose that will change the space and earth existence of man.

Many who have studied the planets and stars

recognize this influence is intense and can be helpful or harmful. They have their equations of what the influence can do, will do or has been doing, but that seems to be the limit of those who study the stars and planets. They believe certain vibrations will cause good or bad prospects and opportunities, and control lives. People see the effects, but very few do anything about them.

The average man who puts his finger in a flame learns it does not feel good and does not put his finger in a flame again. The lesson is, when you know things are not good for you, do something about it. If you get angry and you know it is not good for you, don't blame it on the planets unless you will do something about it. Influence goes both ways. If your health is poor and you blame it on the influence, or know it is the influence, do something to change it. Everything is up to you. The planets don't do anything to change it.

There are two selves of you to act. One self decides how he wants it done and the other is willing to have it done according to the laws and orders of the Higher Self. When you can't stand something don't blame the planets or other people, look within yourself and do something about it. I speak to all of you concerning your own dispositions. Nobody can do anything about them but you. When you can see in others something that is not good or right, and you do not like it, you have it within yourself. So do something about it.

If you expect God to work with you, then you must make your temple ready for God to work in you. Your temple is your thinking mind. Get your thinking mind in order. Clean out the clutter of worldly things and beliefs, only you can make this change. You do not have a long time because the world in general, and the earth in particular, is making a change which no man can stop.

It is important that you talk over your mistakes, misunderstandings, and inability to accomplish your desires. The main reason God gave you a voice was to talk over your troubles with the Angels that have been put in charge of you. It is not enough for any of you to know how or what you believe a thing is. Unless you become a part of it, there will be no affect for you. It remains like blank space. If you expect your mental earth mind or your God mind to grow, you must converse, communicate and have conversations with those who have charge over you.

If you desire to know something that is not known by earth knowledge or intelligence, communicate with your Angels and Masters, they will reveal it to you. Your Masters give in signs and symbols and not by words. If you make a mistake in interpreting the signs and symbols, it is your mistake not the Master's. When you repeat what you have seen, visioned or dreamed, what you say may all be true, or perhaps it may not be true. Many who take upon themselves the responsibility of saying what the stars, time of birth, or visions mean, are giving their own interpretation. It is possible for it to be true or false.

Those who have a fixed idea that a certain word, said a particular way means only one thing, have much to learn. The words that you know may not be known in space. In space it is known as the intention and the purpose. If you will spend as much time looking for the purpose as you do finding a word not to your satisfaction, you will be far ahead of where you are today.

If you find yourself criticizing someone, remember you have all been criticized. You have certain faults or shortcomings that you came into this earth life to cleanse and another person has different faults to overcome. Is there any reason why you cannot help each other? You do not help one another when you pick at them. Speak to them in gentle ways and words. I am endeavoring to save all of you time, for it is precious. If you love, love for the goodness, love for the weakness, and you will find God is with you.

Q. The second Master is a personal Master, is that correct?

A. Your first, second, and third Masters are all personal and they are in charge of giving you the opportunity to unfold your pattern. Your first Master understands your pattern, knows your needs, and he sees that you get your necessary opportunities. He will seek them at every advantageous time in your life, when he sees that you are willing to overcome. Your second Master holds all the records that can reveal to you the past, the present, and sometimes reveals to you the needs of the future. Your third Master will find all the personal contacts for you. He will bring those people you have neglected to fulfill your obligation to, or that you can help on a path of light. Your third Master will bring you in touch with them personally through contacts, other than the instruction work. So everyone that you meet in your life, a friend, a short acquaintance, or those who seem to heap upon you more than you can bear, are the blessings of your life.

Q. Would you please explain the star position?

A. The star position is an exercise to balance the energies in your bodies. To begin the exercise; stand facing east, with your legs apart, arms extended out to the side even with your shoulders, your left palm opened and turned upward, and your right palm facing downward and open. In this position the natural and nature forces meet and flow through your hands. The palms of your hands are the channel through which the energies flow.

The star position benefits the aura. It straightens out the substance aura, and places all substance in its proper position to flow normally. It gives the sensation of soothing and release, and when you have that, your mental mind clears. When the mind clears and becomes active in its Thought action, it replaces any damage, and goes back to its normal self. Continued use of this position for five to fifteen minutes, morning and evening, brings a balancing action to the body. This position should not be used for at least one hour after eating as it will curdle the undigested food in the stomach.

Q. I would like to know more about prayer and whether prayer is purely private. What about speaking prayers in turn?

A. I do not feel that you have the right concept of the word prayer. You have heard expressions of words that were intended to impress, not only themselves, but those around them, what they would like God to do or undo. Now, that is not prayer. Prayer is the opportunity that every man has to speak the words of power that will change any unsatisfactory conditions for the better.

Prayer opens the way for gratitude and thankfulness to be released from the heart center, and is the only time this center has an opportunity to express Godliness. Every man should be willing and ready to express gratefulness, tenderness, thankfulness, and mercy, for all he is capable of coming in contact with, both the invisible and the visible. Speaking the words gives the power to your invisible angels to do what you have expressed, without which, they cannot do.

If you have no desire to speak the words, then you are lacking in yourself. Man's voice was given to him so that he could put into action what the heart feels. We cannot say for any man to do what he does not desire to do, but we would urge all people to learn to desire to pray. No one should ever be ashamed to voice out loud what he knows is in his heart. If he admits he cannot pray, is ashamed to pray before others, or has not the desire to pray for others, his heart surely must be empty, and his words would be empty things.

Never set prayer aside. Never be afraid to pray over the slightest condition of your daily life or for the joys, gratitude, and protection given for your use. When you pray or are alone, do not be afraid to speak aloud, for the spoken word is the power you have to create action. No one can pray too often. You should never be afraid for others to know you pray. When you give thanks to God, you do not have to describe all of the things you are thankful for. When you need something that you are praying for, you do not have to describe it to God, all you need is to know that you are sincere.

Q. What does it mean, "Pray ye one for another?"

A. There is a true meaning that belongs to this physical body; you should pray that the invisible self, your Higher Self, shall always have control, meaning the God Mind over the mortal mind. You cannot avoid your experiences, but if you pray for the physical body to be strengthened, you will be able to take on the trials and tribulations of your pattern.

It also means to pray for those who need help, as your family, friends, acquaintances, those who are searching for Truth, and those in your same association, even to nations, tribes, or peoples of the earth. When you speak your words in prayer, it is the reflection of your desires. In this way you send your Helpers, Masters, and Angels, on their way to do the deed you recognize is necessary for the good of your fellowman. Your prayers are certainly the expression of your Soul, or at least they should be. It is often repeated: the answer is there before you ask. This is true, but asking opens the channel for the manifestation of it. You should rejoice when you pray, and remember, songs of praise are prayers.

Q. Could you please explain the best way to meet the New Year?

A. At the end of the year you are given the opportunity to reminisce over the things you have done during the year. Now is the time to close the book, and remove from the record what you have failed in or should have done, but you did not. Set them aside, they will not leave you. Now, close the book to the records of all that you have finished and let it be forgotten.

When you open up your New Year, those things you have set aside as incomplete should be the first thing on your records to be resolved. Write them down as one, two, three, etc.; and if you determine to make good on them, you will find that almost daily, you can complete one, until you have a clean slate, or a clean program to start out on. If you approach the coming year with the understanding to finish the old and take up the new, fresh energy will come when your strength ebbs low.

You must realize that the New Year can never take place as a new opportunity, as long as you hold on to the old. Think seriously over the past year. What did you fail in that you personally can recognize? Take that into the temple of your conscience. Seek understanding of how to complete it. Each one who has these problems in his record will soon erase them, because the old has no command over the future, and the future has no holding power over the past. The problem is face to face with you: until you do something about it, it cannot move.

There is something dynamic about beginnings. There are all kinds of possibilities in the new year. This is why so many people determine to make a new start the first of every year and resolve to improve themselves. There is a difference between a person who can gradually bring about changes for the better in his life and one who is just satisfied to go along from day to day. It is the strength or weakness of the desire to change, and it is Hope.

Hope is a stimulant to all and a blessing from God. Never let its light grow dim or flicker low. Keep your hope ablaze so you can see a future in which every individual is free to develop along any line they wish, as long as they injure no one else. This way everyone can contribute to life what they love best, and what they do best. The desire to fill a more effective role in life, if it is strong enough, will cause you to leave behind forever, the habits that bar your progress.

Q. Is it true that unless you have forgotten a thing, you have not really forgiven it?

A. Have you forgotten what you forgave your brother? You have never forgiven him if you remember what you forgave. Many are those who say, "I forgive. I will pay no more attention to it. I do forgive, but I'll never give him a chance to do it again." Those people are telling you they have not forgotten. You cannot forgive and remember, for when a karmic debt is balanced between two people, when it is paid, there is nothing to remember. There is a feeling of unshadowed love on both sides.

If you remember an injury or a slight, it is always there in picture form in your mind, and you cannot think of that person without living through distressing sequences again, and again. As long as there is a record in memory, forgiveness is not real. The one who is to be forgiven will know without a doubt when forgiveness is genuine and complete.

Q. Why is it in the spring so many people feel differently about the new season? There is a thrill that doesn't come at the start of other seasons.

A. Every human being on earth experiences the four seasons, even in a tropical climate. As springtime comes, the physical body, in harmony with the rhythm of the world, will long for better conditions than in the past. Now the body cannot think by itself, but responds to the thinking employed by each one in their mental world. If someone is expecting the best of the year, branching out, flowering, the awakening of all things on earth, then his body will respond to his thinking. If he closes his eyes to the beauties of the earth, and the new life that comes each spring, he passes over the best part of life. He is missing another chance to grow, and spring does not come for him, since he is holding onto the dead of winter.

In the winter, a tree is not dead. The sap has gone down to its roots. As soon as the spring appears in the ether, air, and ground, the sap of the tree rises throughout its trunk and branches. In the darkness, the fruit is planned for the coming year. While you do not see a change in the essence that flows in your body, a change is there. The blood stream changes as it awakens and comes forth with new life, so that your whole body can change as the tree does. The only thing man needs to remember is not to interfere with the rejuvenation of his body by thinking of old troubles or ways. In spring, man should see new growth with his eyes, hear nature calling with his ears, and allow his mental equipment to act the same way.

When man feels spring within him, then his thoughts must respond. His words will be words of kindness that make people feel the essence of the flowers, or the fragrance that rises when they walk upon grass. He will express words that will correct what is wrong, and show kindness to those who cannot give kindness. He should listen carefully to words that bring cheer and joy, and close his ears to words of sadness, hurtfulness or that cause confusion. Man is now in the place where he must learn for himself, and there will not always be time for him to learn.

Even if man thinks he is a failure, let him start out again and forget all harms, injuries, hurt feelings, tedious work and miseries. As he looks forward to something greater, his thoughts change, as does his Soul environment. If it is spring for his body and thoughts, then it is spring for his Soul, and he has the great opportunity to work out his problems and clear away mistakes made in the past. There is spring for everyone. It is not exclusive to a certain group, it is for all life. It shows in the fowl, animals, trees and plants, it shows in everything around you. So look forward, for February is the month of incubation that sets what the future will hold.

Q. What is the significance of nature in regards to the Easter time?

A. Springtime is more important for making changes in your life than New Year's Day. The promises and vows made on the New Year seldom last longer than one or two months. At Easter time, you have everything to point the way. All of nature will show you that spring has come. It is in the air you breathe, and the very water you drink. You feel it in the home, in business and in all that you meet. At the time you have these feelings, you can most successfully make a change in your individual life. Changes made between the winter and summer, will work better than if you wait and take any other time of year for your change. The reason is the light rays work upon the mentality of man and are of greatest importance. If man is open to the newness of spring he can respond with great understanding.

Since the highest in man shall ascend, let it become a reality by seeing how much greater the life can unfold in this season than ever before. Let the Ascension mean to man his willingness to change, no matter how satisfied he is with mortal life. Those who approach the Easter season should indeed recognize that it is the inward self of each man that has been crucified and is seeking its freedom. So man should learn that he, too, has seasons with an opportunity every seven years to ascend. If he is willing for this to happen, he has given up nothing. He may assemble all of himself together in perfect wholeness, so there may be a place to receive the instructions of the Higher Self.

Let the flower perfumes that you recognize as essence, go forth and give to all, the sweetness of taking the Holy Breath. Let the beautiful blooms of the Easter lilies symbolize thoughts that have been used for good upon earth. Lilies are like the singleness of purpose that lifts its head and stands straight for all to see. The rose in all its beauty represents the Soul of man, and speaks silently of those rays God sends to earth to help mankind. They silently affirm that GOD IS.

There are hundreds of Seraphim and Cherubim upon the earth who protect the plants, flowers, trees, and grasses. Likewise the angels that are in charge of mankind are sent to protect the Christ Essence in each man on earth. Easter represents another chance for man to unfold that Christ within himself. Not by dying on a cross, but by becoming a living example, as a Son of God. Too much has been said about the Christ Who died upon the cross and too little has been said about the Christ Who lives in every man. At Easter time there is a spring awakening for every man, woman, and child, if they will listen.

Q. Can you give me some direction that will help me develop my spiritual gifts and my higher centers?

A. When I speak of spiritual intelligence I speak of God Mind which is the sum total of all your previous life experiences. Worked out as principles, this Truth pours down upon you as your spiritual intelligence, like a power of light. In physical intelligence you seek to realize and become conscious of your spiritual intelligence, your power of states of Consciousness.

True development comes through the right use of principles, not rules. Rules are an application of a memory habit. Principles are creative in action, while mental rules are contacted by thinking. Rules are worked out by the cause of habit and the effect of your memory. Principles are brought through your Thought force, because Thoughts are already created perfect. You then find you already have the answer without the work of your mental memory. This is power, not mental memory.

Principles of the God Power have been with man since the time of his creation. Principles do not belong to anyone as a possessive act, and they must be used wisely to obtain a true result. I will name some of the principles and if you will study them to know if you have the correct meaning to use them, then you can depend on their goodness. Always remember there are two ways to use principles. The right way will give you the hearing and vision, and the use of the gift you are to use. If you only use them now and then, when you feel like it, you will have misinterpretations, and of course, the false and misleading power.

Love, harmony, responsibility, mercy, kindness, unselfishness, selflessness, and peace are some of the principles you need to study first to understand their true meaning, and find if you have rid your mind of the acts of wrong use. When you are ready to relax and study the proper use of these principles, find a quiet place to do so. While in this mood, do not tell the God Power that you have the right meaning and have been using them, so that all that is necessary now is for the Great God Power to descend upon you. What you need to say and think is, "I am now willing and thankful that I can receive that which is for my right use. Grant that I may understand, Amen." A principle is the head law, and can be used for both good or evil.

Love is the whole of everything: essence, prana, and mind. All creation is perfect in the beginning. Man does not see the beginning, he usually sees only what he interprets as perfection. To know love, man needs to go back to the beginning. This is done through the Spiritual Mind, as it unfolds for man's use.

Harmony means that you agree with God's plan. It does not mean that you agree with all those around you, as to their ideas or work. It does mean that you do not interfere with others as they work out their pattern, and that you do not try to impose your thoughts or beliefs on them. When you use Harmony, you make yourself ready to receive God's Truth. Only then, will Love flow through your life.

Responsibility has a true meaning that is very important. First, unless you are capable to take your own responsibility of life and understand what is expected of you in its fulfillment, you are not ready to use any gift that may be given or developed. Responsibility should begin by taking care of yourself, and helping others around you. Responsibility should not see evil alone, but should see how one can overcome evil. Don't tell others how to overcome evil until you are first the overcomer.

Mercy is one of the greatest assets man can possess. Mercy is the ability of understanding what is right or wrong in action. Mercy does not mean that you should weep with others over things that may be wrong. Mercy means that in your heart you weep because they needed the lesson to be the worker of Truth. Let your mercy be like an unspoken prayer.

Kindness is not a pretense so that others may not know your inner thoughts. It is not doing those things that you feel must be done for others because it is your duty to do it. Kindness is being able to see the need and doing it for your own good. Realize, that when you have an opportunity to do a kindness, it is for your own benefit and others are giving you the opportunity to learn your own lesson.

Unselfishness in action is really about being selfless. This true meaning is one of the hardest steps to take. You must think deeply upon this meaning because it is the purpose before the cause, that produces the effect, or true result. Give and share with others. When you give food, clothes, or your wealth, give something that has power with it, or your most valuable possessions. Now I do not mean for you to go out and give to the first person you contact, but give when you see the true need. When you give, never give when you anticipate what you may receive in return for your gift. This is selfishness in action.

Honesty must be lived because it is your nature of

understanding the law. Because you understand honesty as a law, does not give you the right to condemn others for not being honest. When you can fully understand the word Honesty, it is not a habit, but a pure desire of righteousness. At some time during your past incarnations, you have been dishonest in order to have earned the Truth lesson now. Be patient with others as they learn their lesson. Lying is another form of dishonesty.

Peace is the most misunderstood word in the English language. Peace is all the laws in agreement, in action, in and through you. Peace does not give the right for you to change things that happen around you, which you do not agree with. Peace only comes in your heart and mind, so that you can live it and use it. When you live it and use it, those around you will follow the valuable example. Peace does not come because you tell God how you desire that He should make it come. Peace comes only when you can understand God's plan. So, cease worrying about God's plan and begin forming the real peace within your own life. When the feeling comes to you, "God is in the heavens, and all is well with my Soul", you will have found the true meaning of peace and will be able to live it so all can see. True silence is peace. It is not the amount of words said, but the golden silence of peace in action.

Prosperity is not the worldly wealth you store as treasures. I am sure you have heard this as a sermon many times. Now is the time you should be putting the true meaning into action in your daily life. Do not try to count your good deeds, for this distracts from the value for your own good. Never tell others what goodness you have done. Nothing is of value to you unless you can go over and over, without tiring, the steps which have guided you on your Path of Light. When a lesson becomes tiresome, then you have not learned its Truth.

Truth is the whole of everything.

If you are seeking your Higher Self, if you desire to see visions, or hear the Angel's voice, give your full attention to these laws of Truth. They are of no value unless you use them daily. Study yourself first, so you may be able to help your fellowman. Then you are ready to serve as you seek. Give to your Higher Self your time and energy, then you will receive, not now or then, but all the time. Don't tell God what you want Him to give you; you already have your gift. All you need to do to use it, is open your mind to Truth. Do not look for spirit messages, or to be able to tell other people's fortunes. This is not the true gift, and may be false and misleading to others. Be sure of what you receive, for first you must know the Truth to find your own freedom. You must be led first, before you can lead others.

19

SPIRITLAND

"My Soul greets thee. My heart is filled with Love for all fellowmen. I shall speak words of Truth, giving praise to God on high. Amen. Amen. Amen."

There are five spheres of spiritland that extend into the earth, from the surface down. Begin at the surface as zero degree latitude and the first five spheres extend into the earth from that point. Each of these spheres are divided into seven realms or seven planes. In the very beginning of the spheres, in the lowest position, deep within the earth, begin the earthly planes. In the first one, those preparing to come upon the earth learn how to make a physical body. It takes all the steps of the first sphere to make a suitable pattern for a physical body.

Next they enter into the second sphere and learn how to sustain that body, both in the physical visible and physical invisible condition. They learn about the motion of the visible body and how to feed it solid or liquid food. They learn while in the invisible body that they must exercise their thinking ability to keep it on a path. They realize their form is both visible and invisible.

In the third sphere they begin to develop their five physical sense faculties. This is where they learn how things operate on the solid physical side of life. When they are on the other side, they understand how it repeats itself. They develop their senses to help guide them. This is not the same as the instinct that you find in the animal life.

When they are capable of entering into the fourth sphere, they become responsible for their thinking faculty. They understand how to express, learn the results of desires, and learn to feed the body as it is guided by appetite. So in the realms of the fourth sphere, they come in contact with the worlds of desire, habit, and appetite, which they did not have before. They learn the use or misuse of habits which brings them to the fifth sphere, when they learn the right use of these habits.

In the fifth sphere they learn for the first time that they do not pass from one body into the other as they have in the prior regions of spiritland. They must now come upon the earth to make a change, to demonstrate the desire world in the visible physical body, and they do not care about the penalty of its misuse. This is where they learn that the word "world", means limitation or a boundary. They learn that certain actions will produce the seven steps of death. They can choose which kind of death they are going to have, which they choose for adventure. This is their first opportunity upon the earth surface, where they are able to get in touch with human experience.

They realize they can torment and make life miserable for those who care for them, and they do not hesitate to do it. These newcomers go back and forth from earth to the fifth sphere, by living in a flesh body, dying, and returning to spiritland below the earth. Gradually, as they come into the physical life, they are inspired to become an individual MORTAL human being. At this point they are given the contact between the lower and the Higher Mind where they are guided on their own pattern of individuality. All this takes place before they can move beyond the five spheres within the earth.

Every two thousand years, children are let loose from the lower spheres of spiritland, to take on a physical life, and prove whether they can advance to the state of the mortal human being or not. As you look around, you can see there are many who do not advance. Some of the children coming to earth since the second world war, are entering earth life for the first time directly from the fifth sphere of spiritland.

The next two spheres of spiritland are above the earth. Some mothers from the sixth sphere, come into life to care for fifth sphere children and give them proper training. These children that are little wild beings, are put in charge of their mothers to cultivate, evaluate, and teach them. They must learn about the cultures of physical attainment and cultivate their Spirit to rule over them. They need proper guidance because it is the first time that they have an opportunity to earn a Soul attachment.

Often when they speak of the new age, they are referring to the children coming from the fifth sphere, to take on their Soul pattern as an individual. Many are not getting a good start, and will have to live their lives over and over again, in order to find the parent or mother who will teach them correctly. Any mother who is selfish enough to let her children grow up in ignorance of the Truth of God, may have to come back as a child herself, over and over, until she learns the selflessness of the Christness.

When mothers take on a physical body called the cross, they should be able to give up their selfishness and greed. To love children only as parents, but not to train them, is not what God teaches. As I look around at the parents today with their young children, my heart aches for the child. Yes, we have heartaches here, when we see our beloved students doing the very thing that is harmful to them, and harmful to the children they love. Our hearts ache for their lack of understanding. How great is the Soul of a mother, when she has put forth every effort to teach her children not only the mannerisms of the earth, but also the culture of the Spirit. To cultivate a child's growth and see it produce results, indeed gives great joy, and brings freedom to the parent.

Now many of the children that are coming from the fifth sphere, will enter into the sixth sphere of spiritland above the earth at this time of death, for they are proving themselves to be most worthy of it. There are also those who still act like wild beasts or worse than the wild beasts. It is the beastly nature that they enter into again, in the fifth sphere of spiritland. Until these people can work out of the beastly natures of torture, hindering, harming, destroying, and wanting to be the rulers of man, they will return to the fifth sphere.

There are thousands of the evil forces that you call entities who find satisfaction in living over battlefields, in seeing families suffer, and find great satisfaction in torturing. The God of love we teach you about, did not create them. A lower god of power created the evil disposition of certain types of people. These people must outgrow it by being born many times and repeat the experience until they learn the higher way. There are certain types of people in your own country, even close to where you live, that are quite capable of cruelty and torture. You may think it is impossible for them to do these things, but it is not, and they are making a pattern they cannot escape from. They will eventually outgrow it by going through the many persecutions that men have on earth, to find their Higher Self.

The moment you see something that is not Godly or pure of heart and mind, you can call on the God Powers to take over. Ask God to take that being to a place where he can be taught. Have mercy, for when he passes through this life into the next life, he will go into the fifth sphere of spiritland to suffer the tortures that he has caused on earth. There he will remain until he repents, sees clearly, wants no more of what he has caused, and asks sincerely for forgiveness. Through this repentance and request, he can be lifted out of the beastly nature, because this is the only way he will ever get out of the fifth sphere. Thousands everyday are passing into that sphere, where they must go through the tortures called hell, the pit of torment. They go through the torment they caused on earth, every hour of the day and night. Eventually they work out of this, and when they do, they enter into the sixth sphere of spiritland, above the earth, where man begins his education in reality.

The Hall of Learning is what the college is called in the sixth sphere of spiritland, where they learn their responsibilities as they come to earth. The advancement of the sixth and seventh spheres are above the earth and extend out into all of the atmosphere around the earth, which is the limit of spiritland.

If a man has cheated another man, he does not go into the pit of hell, he goes into the School of Knowledge in the sixth sphere. Through the School of Knowledge, he learns what it means to take from others. Whatever he has taken from others will be taken from him, not in his wealth or possessions, but out of the material substance from which he has to make another body. Sometimes it takes thousands of years to outgrow this, and he will have to wait to come back on earth until he has enough substance to make his body, and prove he has outgrown his cheating nature.

Spiritland is in the invisible side of the third dimension, with the exception of the sixth and seventh planes of the seventh sphere, which extends into the fourth dimension. There are only two spheres above the earth and each has seven planes. Into the sixth sphere enter all who have not evolved to a place that they can finish their pattern, without returning to the earth many times.

In the sixth sphere, there are seven planes. In the first planes are those who are struggling, and they believe it is by the educational program that they can fit themselves to overcome life's problems. Let us call them the complainers. They always tell you that another way is best, or someone else could have done it better, or they could have made it perfect. They are struggling to understand life's problems.

From the third, fourth and fifth planes of the sixth sphere, you will find those who have been touched by love, love of family, mother, father, children, family activities, and worldly possessions. They seek to have more and more, for they have not learned that wealth cannot buy or secure heavenly rewards.

In the sixth and seventh planes of the sixth sphere are those who have received the great educational abilities that are open to the peoples on earth. They sometimes become the great poets, painters, the great machinists, or tradesmen of the day. They can change the systems and social abilities of the earth, and assist the awakening of the peoples by being reincarnated over and over again.

Some have come to the first, second, or third plane, by living many lives on earth, yet have not learned the beginning lessons. They have not learned that individuality is responsible for being connected with the quickness of Soul, the Christness of you.

The fallen angels came on earth, to help those in the

sixth and seventh spheres of spiritland. They came into bodies and helped enough so that when man entered into spiritland of the sixth sphere, he could see the mistakes and recognize his responsibility of putting things in order for advancement. Those that were the fallen angels also found themselves entering into the seventh sphere, because they had made their own mistakes. They had to work out the generations of the seventh sphere, where you take on your spiritual generation. The sixth sphere is where you take on your mortal advancement in the generations.

Those who have become weary of life's possessions, social activities, and the educational program, know there is something higher, and have awakened to the Christness within themselves. They are in the first, second, and third planes of the seventh sphere. There they enter into the College or School of Wisdom. While the sixth sphere holds the School of Learning, the seventh sphere holds the School of Experiences that produces wisdom as a result.

Those on the sixth and seventh plane of the seventh sphere of spiritland are aware of the fourth, fifth, sixth, and even the seventh dimension, but they have no control over them. They do not know how to ascend yet to another dimensional condition. In the space about twenty five miles from the earth is where you will find the sixth and seventh spheres. As long as man departs from his earth life, and does not enter into the sixth or seventh plane of the seventh sphere, he will be subject to rebirth on earth.

Remember, that if there are no births today, twenty years from now those in spiritland will not be able to return to life on earth. There will not be the opportunity to overcome, or to learn, for where will they be born? Great changes began to take place on your earth when mothers forgot to nurse their own babe. These children were nursing the nature of animals, and not the Spirit mother who gave them birth. Here is where the change took place, and where roughness, crudeness, and inharmony, is continuing on earth today.

When you advance enough so that you have no physical connection, and nothing below the Soul development, you will then ascend into the Kingdom of the Elohim. You have been many thousands of years, coming as far as you have from the human kingdom, into the MORTAL human kingdom. When what you recognized as the Adam age came, this was the time many took on the Mortal human kingdom body, and before that time it was not connected.

When you leave the mortal human kingdom, you will enter the space that is between the Angel Kingdom and the Elohim Kingdom. It is not what is above you as ether, for that space is not the same. That is why we teach about the dimensions instead of the space around the earth. The space around your earth is called your universe. The kingdoms are part of the existence of the universe just as you are part of the universe. Amen. Amen. Amen.

20

KNOW WHAT YOU SEEK

"My Soul greets thee. My heart is filled with Love for all fellowmen. I shall speak words of Truth, giving praise to God on high. Amen. Amen. Amen."

How great are your desires? Are your desires beyond the material world? As I and many Light Bearers work close to the earth plane, we see a great need for explaining the misunderstanding of the true meanings of the words you use everyday. Words such as love, heart, and spirituality are three misleading terms that need to be recalled to your conscious mental mind.

On earth the word love, as used today, means companionship, free use of passion and mating. All this is purely physical if you stop to think about it. Even parents' love turns to physical possession. At birth the child is held close to Spiritual love, but as the child grows, the Spiritual love turns to physical action. Parents turn to the Spiritual action only in times of need. The Spiritual answer is then expected immediately, but most often the answer or result is too slow, because in the material time not enough Divine Essence has been created. DIVINE ESSENCE is the substance from which All things are created upon the earth. It is essential that all seekers examine what kind of love they possess, and are using.

The heart is a vital organ in your body. Without its

power the body cannot act in Nature's way. So when you speak of the heart within and how you feel concerning life, you are not using any power of action except nature power. Truly, as God created you, He also gave you the ethereal heart, which is the Center that controls the power of nature. It is spiritual action when it is not interfered with in its performance of duty to natural health.

The beat of the heart is controlled by man's thinking ability. "As a man thinketh, so is he." When you hear the word heart used as the center of your being, you mean to think and say it is the ethereal heart center of your true consciousness or God Being of life. This is where all Truth and all divine essence controls your Spiritual Heart Center, which is your God Mind Consciousness. It does not control your nature pattern, but only the natural power over the visible and invisible performance of all life connected in your life pattern. When you speak about the heart center, you mean the Thought center of your consciousness.

When you are speaking of your heart within the physical body, you are in the thinking center of your consciousness. Think much about your heart within. You can quiet your heart action by being still. Sometimes this is done by less action of your body or by less action of your thinking. This means not recognizing physical things not yet possessed, or what you think is yours by possession. You will soon see this is a limitation of your Heart Center, the thinking consciousness. In the consciousness of your Divine Heart Center, there is no limitation.

Spirituality is when you have divine love in your consciousness, as your ethereal heart center. Of course it will work upon the heart organ in your physical body. You can recognize it working by your pulse action. Just think about something joyful, and watch your pulse action. You will see that when you are doing good deeds and thinking of desirous actions of selflessness, your physical heart will beat smoothly and never cause pain.

When joy enters in the action of life, you will be lifted up into the Thought Realm of divine essence. Your physical heart will seem to overflow, but without any notice of pain. You will be lifted up above the world of material life. In fact, you will be in the action of Invisible Power, where all true things exist before they appear on earth. Isn't this what every sincere seeker desires? The light within is the consciousness of the higher Thought Realm. The higher light is the realization of Truth.

If you are seeking light, you will need to understand it is not the posture of the body, or the words you repeat, that bring you light. It is the attitude of your thinking mind that brings you peace, love and spiritual growth. No teaching or method of development can work, unless you are willing to do the work of knowing what you seek, how you seek, and how to use it when you do receive it. Many people want Truth, but when they receive it, they do not want to use it unless they are praised for their result. They feel they must show off, and this is an example of casting pearls uselessly.

In the Bible, it tells where the fishermen were on the troubled sea, and they found the Great Teacher asleep. These words tell you a true story. The sea translated means Thoughts. The sea was troubled by confusion, so they called the Great Teacher to work for them. When He calmed their thinking consciousness, they saw the Light and were saved. No one will have trials, confusion, or be misled if they will turn to the Higher Consciousness. What they will find is Peace and Truth, not by outer actions, but through the True Heart Center of Life.

Illumination of the Spiritual Mind is not acquired

when you feel it is your appointed time, but comes only when you are ready for it. Spiritual illumination cannot be put aside and used only when it pleases you to use it. What you need is selflessness. Your illumination is there for you to see, understand, and use. It is never away from you; only you can close the door between your God Mind and your thinking mind. Each seeker needs to open their thinking mind to reality. This comes by seeking to understand the great difference between the material things of earth; those things which have solid form, shape, time limitation, direction, expansion, and contraction. They must seek to reach the Natural things, invisible to nature's creation.

All scientists use their inner sight, even though they may not call it that. It tells them what is needed and how it is possible. It is an image in their Thought consciousness, and they become aware of it. They believe this image and it stays with them day and night until they do something about it. It is very important to remember, to keep on working or striving for the image for your mental mind to think upon. Always be willing to strive for the greater performance. Don't strive to grasp changes of growth in your thinking world all at once. Take one step at a time remembering what you understand today may be enlarged upon tomorrow. What you receive today is what you can understand, and pushing ahead, may bring mistakes.

When the Great Teacher taught to turn within, it was to listen to the Higher Mind, where the images are real and true. What seems to stand between the true spiritual conception of Truth and the material or worldly consciousness, is the mixed interpretations of words. It pays to seek the true meaning of the words you hear and read. If your thinking consciousness can perceive an Image by desiring peace, love and spiritual growth, then your consciousness will expand upward to the Thought consciousness, where the conception of true reality dwells forever. What great joy and peace will pour over your entire being when you can recognize the full meaning of Love as Jesus Christ knew it.

Being humble does not mean to lay aside your dignity and present understanding. It means laying aside all false thinking and superstitions, and being true to your self to the best of your knowledge. Seek and desire to know what you are thinking, and the answer will be given to you. You will know what is hindering your success. Thinking will keep you down or lift you up until you reach your goal of illumination. If you make yourself willing to listen to the still, small voice within, you will unfold by a true guidance that will never fail you.

In meditation, it is necessary to use your thinking mind to know what you are seeking. It is common acceptance in the world of the physical man, that he has five physical senses, hearing, seeing, tasting, smelling, and the last or fifth sense, feeling. You cannot use hearing, seeing, tasting or smelling, without the use of the sense of feeling. You can however use the sense of feeling without any of the first four senses. So it is possible that the action of feeling can be the door to the higher faculties. How you use feeling can be the cause between knowing and not knowing the Truth.

Actions of peace, love, and calmness, or hate, evil, and confusion, are connected to the feeling sense. Emotions and sensations are not the actions of the sense of feeling. Emotions and sensations act upon the glands and vital organs in the trunk of your physical body, while the sense of feeling acts upon the nerve centers of your whole body. This produces your ability of being conscious of thinking Truth. May the God Power guide and direct you on your path of illumination. Amen. Amen. Amen.

21

THE EARTH'S UNIVERSE

"My Soul greets thee. My heart is filled with Love for all fellowmen. I shall speak words of Truth, giving praise to God on high. Amen. Amen. Amen."

In this discourse I shall continue to expand out into space. Man needs to bring to his consciousness, more understanding of what is meant by the term Space, and to be more aware of how close the space is connected with this physical earth. Man should be willing to study and realize how great a work he is given, to get closer to his Divine Self.

No one should be so delighted with their personal appearance that they would overlook this body representing the Temple of God. One of the first principles is to maintain and present the body in a manner that respects the body as the Temple of God. "Know ye not that all men are Gods?" This Bible quotation, spoken by a great Teacher, taught that all men should be free by knowing the Truth.

There is no way to prove anything to man, even though it may be in the solid material world. One needs to know all to have a Truth. That which is in your thinking mind, is only a picture of Thoughts and Ideas. When thinking on the level of Thoughts and Ideas, it is like another world, which your physical senses cannot see. According to the ability man has to reach out from his body, he can realize his use of the several states of consciousness to know a Truth. A proven Truth to one person may not be accepted as Truth by others. The truth may not be complete, but can be in the process of manifestation as a whole Truth or condition. Try to realize this statement, "All things are possible."

Imagine that you are working in a great chemical laboratory, where many experiments are going on over and over, until the exact action has been found that proves the result. Yet until the last test or experiment had been made, they were not sure of anything. They believed, and had the faith to seek the Truth by experiments, until it was a Truth. So it is with all new things that you think about, but do not understand. The Truth is there and can be explained, but you are the one who must have the Faith and believe to the end. When at last you do understand, only then will you see how simple it has been for you to find that Truth for your benefit. When you have a Truth it will never leave you, and it will thrill you every time you use it or think about it. This is progress and is man in evolution.

When you seek too much at one time, like trying to consume a book of wonderful Truths, you cannot call this learning for Truth's sake. It is simply reading and believing you understand what you read. You may know the words you are reading, but do you know the true meaning intended by the writer of the book? This type of learning will never stay with anyone, for you cannot see and know what manifestations the writer had to establish the foundation of their written words. Each one needs his own experience, and I will keep impressing this upon you, until you can read your own Book of Life. When you progress too fast, you cannot digest what you need to know and remember. We teach man seeking his own path of Light, to travel his path slowly. Thereby he will not become weary and discouraged only to fall by the wayside, sometimes not to rise again in this life.

There are many meanings to almost every word in the English language, and each meaning has its particular use. To find workable Truth, you cannot see for one day, or occasionally, as the mood suits you. Truth is put together day by day, piece by piece, experience by experience, until you can look at the whole and understand its great meaning. There are many paths of Light to be traveled. No matter which path man seeks, he will arrive in time, for there is but one Truth. No man is ever lost to God, but he may get lost in his understanding of God. Each man should choose the path of Life that he can best follow to get understanding.

Scientists will tell you there is much beyond the stars and where each star is located. For the scientist to tell you what he may know, will not help you unless you also make the constant effort to know for yourself. Scientists may encourage or entice you until you willingly make the effort to know for yourself. They know that as long as you listen or view their picture you are making an effort for your own benefit, but the scientist cannot portray the whole truth of his understanding to you. Like the scientist, you must study patiently and never weary that you do not come to the end, for there is no end to life or learning.

You have a number of bodies and each one of these bodies work together at the same time, yet you only see the outer shell of the physical body. I will tell you about your seven bodies, and how each one is connected to this physical body. It may cause you to do much thinking to find a solid foundation for more understanding. Perhaps you are thinking there seems to be too many bodies to think about. Let me assure you it is something wonderful to know what you are, and where you fit into the great beyond of Earth's Universe.

Many men have said, "How I wish I knew more about the stars. Where is that deep that the stars show through to us down here on earth?" Have you ever said this? Have you heard where the earth universe begins and where it has its ending? Does it have a limit? I am sure you realize the earth is held in space, but do you know how, or what holds it in space? What brought it all about in the beginning? Let us consider this well, look at it, and think about it. This is done by Thought action and following your own imagination, which is a Mind Faculty of the God Mind.

As you look away from earth you usually refer to it as expanding into space or looking upward. This statement is not always true. When you look toward the sun you may believe this is upward, but this is not always true. Let us look at what is meant by the term space, so you will know why and how you are looking into space. As you stand upward on your feet, it means that your head, the thinking part of you is farthest away from the earth's magnetic action. At times you will be standing upward, towards the sun, but at other times you may actually be standing with your feet toward the sun. No matter how you are standing, you are extending out into space if you are standing on your feet. The earth planet orbiting the sun has nothing to do with your extending out into space.

The earth's universe is a great expansion of space and it does have a limitation or a boundary. For clarity, let us say, that the earth's space is confined in a shell-like container, called cosmic ether, which is the beginning of the earth's law and order. It is the alpha or first. You have been taught that the earth is but one of the planets included in the earth's universe. Which planet was created first no man can correctly say, but he may think he knows.

What exactly is space? When speaking of the contents found within the boundary of the earth's universe, we are speaking of ether. There are three very important words that you should read about in a Webster's Unabridged Dictionary. I will go over some terms for you to think about. Space is an extension, considered independent of anything; also any quantity or portion of extension. Extension is stretching out; expanding; no limit. Deep is being below the surface of anything; descending; low in situation; hidden; secret; not easily understood. These three words are used in your Bible and in our explanation of the Universe around the earth as it sits in space. This universe is filled with a quantity and quality of ether.

It will make it easier for you to follow the next explanation about the universe if you will take a pencil and paper and mark down what I tell you. First in the center of your paper, draw a circle, about one inch in size, and in the circle write, earth planet. Then around this earth circle, draw seven circles of about one-half inch in size. When you have made these seven circles write within them as directed. In the circle closest to the earth, put number one, in the next or second circle put number two, and go on in each circle until you have numbered the seven circles and you will have marked the seven divisions of the universe space. Remember, space contains something, in this case called ether. Begin now to fill in your circles so that you can see more clearly where the changes come, from the highest to the lowest which is the earth. Begin by filling in the circle closest to the earth. (See Chart)

Let us begin with the first division belt, or the lowest ether, closest to earth. This region is filled with air or oxygen, the breath of life. This extension of the air division goes out from the earth about twenty-five miles, and this oxygen is created as quantity and quality for every living thing that is upon the earth. There are no two human or mortal human beings that breathe the same breath of life, as one would like to believe. Everything takes in breath according to their own exact pattern of life. The Natural Pattern, designed by God is perfect. But when the nature takes over it changes according to, "As a man thinketh so is he." By his thinking, he interferes with the Natural perfect breath to one of nature. Soon disease and death is on the breath of life.

It is important to realize that spiritland is in this space extending out from earth. The sixth and seventh spheres of spiritland are in this first belt. There are also five lower spheres of spiritland that are confined within the earth. I would also like to call to your attention the definition of Ether. It is a hypothetical medium of extreme tenuity and elasticity supposed to be diffused throughout space as well as among the molecules of which solid bodies are composed, and to be the medium for the transmission of light and heat; fields of light and ether; and flow.

The second division belt is the action belt of space. In this belt or region the atmosphere is being changed into the lower ether air, for the living things upon the earth. This work is accomplished by action, wind storms, lightning, clouds, rain, mists, snow, and heat or cold waves. The important part of this mixing of air, is the lowering of the amount of atmosphere ether, which is about 90% lower, called the breath of life. Otherwise, man would burn up or be exploded. This is like the medium ether atmosphere. This belt also extends about twenty-five miles out in space beyond the first belt. It is the place of darkness, and it is said, yet I will not verify its truth, that it is the home of the evil forces.

Next comes the third division belt and this is the highest division of the atmosphere of purest ether. This belt extends many miles above the first two space belts, and it is in this belt that all have a difficult time to leave or re-enter the earth. This is the gravity belt. This region or belt contains all that is necessary to make or build the two terrestrial bodies, one that is usually invisible, and the visible, physical, flesh body. Both of these bodies are limited by gravity force. This atmosphere is called the Nest or storing place of all seeds of life in any of the four lower kingdoms. I cannot prove this to you, you need to think about it deeply.

The fourth division belt of ether is called the dense ether belt. This is the place where the seeds of the two lower bodies are created. It is here that man's visible and invisible bodies were planned and created, when the Gods took over creating Adam and Eve, or the new bodies. This is the pattern of creation to make your pattern of life. The Arch Angels work here to mold your body pattern to fit the mind pattern of your Higher Self. Notice carefully, this belt is divided into seven lesser divisions that make one perfect whole.

Let us look at these divisions. The first mixture of life is plasma. This is not the term you recognize as blood plasma. This plasma type is the gathering together of all the materials of quantity and quality that will be joined to make or mold a life on earth. The second mixture is called ectoplasma which represents the shell or holder for the pattern to be created. It is the first seal. The third mixing is called protoplasma and this is the pattern which shall be enfolded as the life pattern of the higher and lower mind, and all qualities of life. The fourth mixing is called the cytoplasma which is the sealing off from the Higher Self, and making a separate individual pattern of life. This is the pulse of anything. It is the nature laws of life joined with the higher Natural Laws of life. God called this His Image and Likeness Man. Thus ended His creation and He rested. The fifth mixing is the beginning of the mortal life bodies, making the bloods that are found in the lower bodies. This is the plasma as the bloods. There are four types of blood in every human being, known as the white, yellow, red, and blue bloods.

The physical part of you calls for four types of blood, and the digestive system must answer the need of each call, acting as one of nature's laws. Your white blood is the creative cell of intelligence and carries the red blood to many parts of your flesh body. It is the most closely connected to the Father of nature in the solar plexus. The red cells carry what is needed to fill the intelligent direction. The red blood builds and repairs the physical man. It is often called the vital water of life for it carries your physical pattern composition. The blue blood creates the substance from which all parts of mind functions, such as the brain matter and the liquid found in the nerves. The yellow blood is found as the marrow of the bone, where cells of the other bloods are created. If there are no creative cells, and no blood of intelligence, then death sets in. The study of the four types of blood is worthwhile to everyone who would like to know more about their own body.

The sixth mixing is where the substance material is formed. This is not the breath of life, but is the prana life of your invisible self. We would like you to remember this body as your shadow self, because it is with you always as you live in this flesh body. You enter into it by your mental mind when you are asleep, and it encircles you while you are awake.

The seventh mixing is the creation of matter, which is germ life. Without germ life the matter substance which you call flesh would not live. The matter carries the vital energy, the sex energy and the spiritual energy, which make you a living man on earth. This is the story told of the Divine Trinity, Father as Essence,

Mother as Prana, and Son as God Mind.

Now we will continue with the fifth division belt which is called the Light Ether. Here is the gathering of all the elements that go into the making of Life as living life seeds. Here you will find the dust of the stars, such as the molecules and atoms that make and sustain living life on earth. In this division of space are the fields and regions that the Lord Gods work in. Here is the creation of the lower mind, so that in time it could be joined to the higher God Mind. This light ether or star dust, is what the sun shines upon that gives to man on earth what is called sunlight.

Next we have the sixth division belt. This is called the Element Belt or rarefied ether, and this is the space where scientists are ever turning to be able to harness powers into forces.

The last is the seventh division belt which is called the Power Ether. It contains law and order, the first two principles of anything.

Perhaps you are thinking there is too much detail here that might seem disconnected from a Spiritual path. But this is a foundation for Spiritual understanding. Perhaps you already know many of these things, but we must reach those who do not know about them. Be patient so that your neighbor may get the foundation and be better able to travel with you. I would like to tell you next about your seven bodies. Amen. Amen. Amen.

Earth Universe Belts

- All of the six bodies of man are created within the earth universe belts.
- The seventh body of man, the I AM, Elohim, Son of God, is created outside of the earth universe belts.
- The first three belts or atmosphere belts surround the earth like a shell. They sit within the dense ether belt that holds them together.
- The story about Adam and Eve in Genesis took place in the dense ether belt.

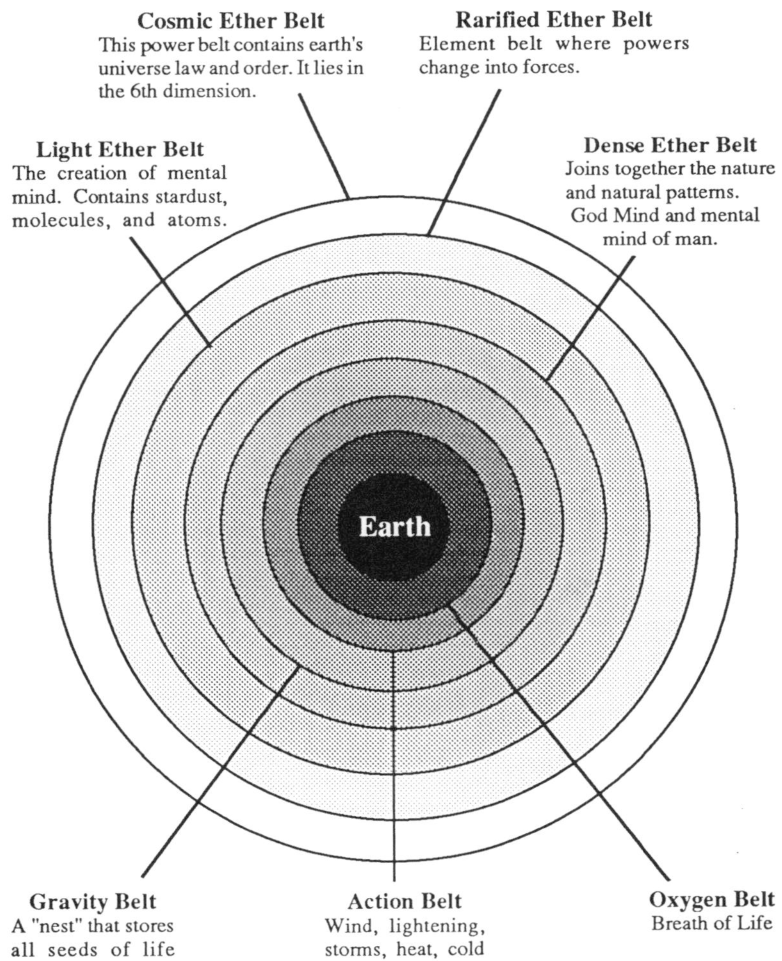

Seven Bodies

1. Physical Flesh Body	Terrestrial elements, lower half of third dimension
2. Physical substance Body	Terrestrial elements, upper half of third dimension
3. Mental Body, or the Ego	Ethereal Elements, lower half of the fourth dimension
4. Spirit Breath Body	Ethereal Elements. Upper half of the fourth dimension
5. The Soul Body	Astral Elements, all of the fifth dimension
6. The Holy Ghost Body	Celestial Elements, all of the sixth dimension
7. The Elohim Body	Celestial Elements, all of the Seventh Heaven, outside of the Cosmic Universe

22

YOUR SEVEN BODIES

"My Soul greets thee. My heart is filled with Love for all fellowmen. I shall speak words of Truth, giving praise to God on High. Amen. Amen. Amen."

You have seven bodies that work together in and through the outer flesh body. I will name them and place them in your universe so that you can think about them in a reasonable pattern. All seven bodies work together at the same time. When you understand them you can recognize what is going on about and within you, and the world that surrounds you. Then you can say that you are a free man and a free thinker, for being unhampered by ignorance is the meaning of freedom.

The simplest way to understand the uses of your different bodies is to watch the results obtained by action. There are two results, personality or individuality. If you are using the material or qualities of your physical life, you will develop personality. If you are using the spiritual qualities of life, your endeavors will bring about spiritual individuality. Either of these qualities can be seen by yourself or your friends.

If God had not intended for man to know about his seven bodies, He would have hidden the knowledge. Throughout the records left for man to study, it is clear that all knowledge, wisdom and understanding is given for man's benefit. Have you ever wondered why the records would speak about the Son of God or the Angels of Light, if God did not intend for man to have this knowledge freely? If God gives to man freely what he needs daily, surely, then, this knowledge of life will be included to meet his needs for greater understanding.

The Bible and many other records show that man gains Spiritual Wisdom according to the interest he employs. Man cannot expect to have his great Spiritual awakening until he shows this wisdom. It so happens that man shows interest for help when he is down and out, or worldly aid to health has failed. This can happen to the mind as well as the body. When there is no where else to turn to seek help, then man will trust in God, even proclaiming that God is the Source of help. How wonderful God never criticizes man, when God and His help is placed second on the list. Truth is everywhere if man will make the effort to find it. It all depends upon the interest of man's will to seek until he does find it.

Where is the benefit if the story of your physical body was all that would be given to you? You live with this physical body and you have the use of your mental mind, and you should know it better than anyone else. All you have to do is make a strong effort to change your ways, especially your thinking, to be the person that in your heart you desire to be. Only through your desiring and longing, can you in time find what is beyond this physical knowledge of your small personal world and its surroundings. Learn to recognize your longings as your urges, and your desires as the inspirations leading you to find those things that are lasting. Then you will have the memories that cannot be disturbed by time.

Beginning with your physical body, you can be shown where each of your seven bodies are connected to this physical body, making one perfect whole. I call attention to things about your physical makeup, because you will need to see them clearly. You do not see what this outer body contains or how it works. This body is where you have all the experiences to make the other bodies stronger in you. Here we find the answer to much disease and ill health. Unless some part of the physical body is not giving good service, or you have discomfort, you seldom pay much attention to the body's need. All the powder and make-up that you can put on your face will never make you healthy. The habit of eating the proper food at the right time, will do more for your beauty and health, and you will enjoy life to its fullest in strength and magnetic attraction, which is the true aim toward perfection.

Perfection is what many say they are seeking and beauty is what each desires that others see in the daily life. Instead of trying to help Nature Laws by looking different from what nature has intended, realize that the Natural Laws precede the Nature Laws. This would mean that all men and women should have a straight, clean, honest look about them, without any covering up by make-up. Man should be accepted for what he is and what he stands for. All this should be reasoned out for each seeker to make their own decisions about which self they desire to serve.

Now I will name the seven bodies for you. The first is the Physical Flesh Body which is composed of the terrestrial elements from the lower half of the third dimension. Second is the Physical Substance Body composed of the terrestrial elements of the upper half of the third dimension. Third is the Mental Body or the Ego, composed of the ethereal elements of the lower half of the fourth dimension. Fourth is the Spirit Breath Body, composed of the ethereal elements of the upper half of the fourth dimension.

Fifth is the Soul Body, composed of the astral elements from all of the fifth dimension. Sixth is the

Holy Ghost Body, composed of the celestial elements from all of the sixth dimension. Seventh is the Elohim Body, composed of the celestial elements from the Seventh Heaven, outside of the cosmic universe. Remember the four Physical Bodies are governed by Nature Laws and the three Spiritual Bodies are governed by the Natural Laws. (See chart)

Let us look at the Shadow Body or Physical Substance Body. You will find in your dictionary the material substances which a body is composed of is called Stuff, but that does not mean God Mind Stuff. The difference in these two actions can be explained. Substance stuff is the Prana creation or chemical action and God Mind Stuff is the Essence of Light. The shadow body is connected to the physical body through the solar plexus, which is in the middle or trunk of your body. It is connected to the body by the silver cord, and it is invisible to the sense of sight. This is the cord that makes all records of your experiences into your Book of Life. This cord is separated from the flesh body at death and takes seventy-two hours to be completely closed.

Around the two physical bodies as one, there is the aura, which can be plainly seen by many and holds all your life pattern together as your universe. This aura contains all the power, force and energy that man needs to keep him upon the earth plane. The Shadow Body is held above the Physical Body at all times, as long as there is life in this Physical Body. The Shadow Body creates your appetites, desires and habits which produces the action for all your needed experience on earth. Thus it is said to control man's will power. All the work of the shadow body comes through the upper half of the third dimension.

Here I will take time to tell you the meaning of the Centaur. It is pictured as half man and half animal, and legend pictures it as an actual race on earth. I would not make conflict with any belief, but here is the Truth. The legend has great meaning in man's creation, for the upper half of the Centaur represents man as the head of God Mind, which is the intelligence or faculties acting through the God Will. The lower half of the Centaur is represented as the horse or animal, and means the nature or nature body. Man is governed by his desires, habits and appetites, thus this would be through the mortal mind, and his senses governed by the ability of reasoning. You have in this legend the explanation of the Nature Law and the Natural Law at work.

The two bodies of the third dimension are held together by life and death. The laws of nature work through the vital organs of man, and the natural laws work through the Mind Ability, giving man the freedom to choose which nature he desires to use. Let all sensible people meet the true conditions of life and never shun hearing this Truth. The Invisible Shadow body creates the Waters of Life, and this fluid is gathered in the ductless glands. From there it is placed in the ganglion glands and on to the vital organs of the body. Life visible and invisible goes on with or without your consent. Life and death is evolution for man.

The Ego body is mortal man's thinking mind, and it has its action on the lower section of the fourth dimension. This is often called the vision realm because it is possible for some to be able to see into this realm, but not with the physical eye sight. It is like imagination working, it is real to mind, but not physically possessive. You see the results of thinking, but you cannot see how you think. The work of the Ego mind is to develop the five physical senses, so that the Reason and Imagination faculties can work for man's good. The Mental Body is governed by the will of man for "As a man thinketh so is he". Let me explain that you have a Golden Cord, that is connected to the seventh center or chakra, which is the head center of Love. It is through this center that the Essence to the Mind passes to the voluntary and involuntary brain nerves of the nervous system. So you have the Silver Cord and the Golden Cord, the mental mind and the God Mind. This is referred to as the Inspirational Force.

The Spirit Body or Spirit Breath is important for the existence in the flesh body. You put the spark of life on every cell through every breath that you draw into your lungs. This is called purifying the blood, for as the blood passes through the arteries and veins, all the spark of life is taken out of the blood cells. Then as it returns to the heart and the new sparks of life and oxygen are placed upon each cell, the intelligence of the Ego body or nature, knows exactly where each cell is needed, and its use. So what you call growth is the constant building that goes on in your body until you pass through the change called death. The Spirit Breath is created from the elements of the upper half of the fourth dimension. Those who claim they have seen the spirit breath at birth say it is pure white in color and that it is a vapor-like substance. Those who claim they have seen it leave the body at death see it as a grayish vapor. At birth it seems to be at the mouth and at death it seems to be at the chest area of the body. The spirit breath is not the Holy Ghost.

The Soul Body is composed of the Astral elements and functions through the God Mind to the mental mind, having its center in the brain portion of the head. The work of the Soul is the communication between the God Mind and the mental mind, and has the work of separating the worldly material things from the spiritual things. This is called the working of the life pattern, and its activities are the actions of man's spiritual and earthly patterns. The Soul uses both the upper and lower divisions of the fifth dimension to keep all records. You have heard of the Book of Life, and this is the meaning if it. When you pass through death, the first knowable thing to take place is that you are shown the records of all that you have failed in called karma or sin. You are also shown what you have overcome.

Here let me tell you a little about what a generation means. You have taken on a certain pattern to work out in life on earth, or in a physical body, and this may take many earth lives to complete. When it is worked out you change to another pattern. This goes on and on until you overcome death, so that you do not need to come back to earth in a physical body. Some people today are in the forty second generation since the Adam creation.

The Soul has all control of the connection to the God Mind, as well as to the mortal mind. Its connections are through the pineal gland, the nerve centers of the physical body, and the Spiritual centers in the head. These are in action controlling the emotions, sensations, vibrations, and the sounds and speed of light. The Soul occupies the whole of the fifth dimension, which is created of the astral elements, and here is the separation of powers into forces. You will find that the aura or universe that surrounds you, controls the Ideas, Thoughts and the ability of thinking. The rays of intelligence are allotted to man by the ability of how he uses his intelligence. The Soul works the All Seeing Eye, the vision that allows man to recognize the past, present and future.

The Holy Ghost Body is the channel through which life takes on the qualities of the earth body, called the pattern of life. This is the sixth body, called the Glory Body, and it occupies the Element Belt of Power, likened to God Power. You will see it as your individuality or likeness of God. In the sixth dimension where earth life begins, much work takes place. This is first the channel for God Mind function where the power is changed into forces; the forces are changed to energies; and the energies are changed to magnetic attraction. Magnetic attraction is the gathering of all essence, prana and mind to one pattern, called life. The essence to flow through the nervous system, the prana to flow through the nature digestive and circulatory systems, and the Mind to flow through the four states of consciousness. All of these first six bodies are created within the Cosmic Universe Belt.

Last we have the Elohim, Son of God Body. This is your Sonship of God Self. This body is created outside of your universe. This is the Star Belt of the Milky Way. Here the Father-Mother Trinity creates the Son. Let us look at this in a reasonable way for better understanding. The Father is the natural and positive; the Mother is the nature and negative; together they begat a Living Son, called Elohim Christ. Here I use the Hebrew word "begat". This is entirely different from the word "born". It means that from the Laws of the Natural and the Laws of Nature, as Essence and Prana, the Gods created a Son, Elohim, and the word Elohim is plural. This Son Elohim was the Mind descending to earth. It was to be made in the Image and the Likeness of the Gods, but in and through the development of man. You will need to think much upon these words, but if you will keep at it, you will see the Light.

The first chapter of Genesis in the Bible tells you the story plainly, but because man has been drilled through many beliefs that are not true, he often hesitates to see the Light when it is before him. Man needs to step forward and take Truth so it may change many conceptions of what he thought was true. False truths do not give true satisfaction to the Soul qualities of the Conscience of Life, connecting the reason for living on earth and the reason for evolution. May the Blessings of the Great White Light be over you. Amen. Amen. Amen.

23

THE KINGDOM OF ANGELS

Because of the great interest in Angels today, we are including this brief work Nola left. Nola wrote this for the students, based on her shorthand notes of June 15, 1933. The notes came from a talk that Phylos gave at their camp on Mt. Shasta.

Strange wonders permeate our world, sublime mysteries almost too pure for our full understanding. Our planet, and its atmosphere is not only pervaded by invisible radioactive waves and silent, potent rays, but by shining beings whose ceaseless works as ministries enliven and uplift us. More wonderful than the far-reaching effects of inventions to come or the harnessing of the inimitable cosmic rays, will be our recognition of these Glorious Presences.

Since time unveiled its amazing creation, Angelic Beings have nurtured the advancement of the unfoldment of man. References to them have usually been accepted with amusement and disbelief. Behind every ageless belief, however, lies a hidden reality whose meaning should be sought with earnestness. Our ignorance of Angels does not make them non-existent, it only closes us to their existence. Our yearning to realize them opens us to their association. God grant that every one may receive a confirmation of their reality.

The Angelic Kingdom, like the Human Kingdom, is a

path of evolving Life. It is composed of beings whose bodies, compared to ours, are etheric. The purpose underlying Angelic unfoldment is perfection through joyousness and service. The human way is impelled toward the development of love and wisdom. Those who inhabit the Celestial Kingdom are free from strife and evil.

Human beings are strengthened by overcoming the forces of discord and malice within themselves. Angels are immortal. Human beings require the rest of death to prepare them for new cycles of self-expression. The way of Angelic evolution is exacting and long, whereas that of human wayfarers, though strenuous, is comparatively short. The more man associates with nature, the purer his vibrations become because Nature beings have no destructive emotions. All is done consciously from the highest and purest levels.

There are numerous Celestial Orders, many of which we know very little about. The groups from whom we receive ministrations are:

1. The Angels of Nature
2. The Builders of Form
3. The Angels of Inspiration
4. The Angels of Love
    a. Guardian Angels
    b. Healing Angels
    c. Religious Angels
    d. Song Angels
5. The Angels of Birth
6. The Angels of Death

The Angels devoted to nature cause a continuous renaissance action in that kingdom. They supervise the elements and the seasons of our year. The law of cause and effect ordains the kind of ministry the earth deserves to receive. They cannot prevent earthquakes or floods, but they can bring rain or calm to a worthy region. When mankind ignorantly or heedlessly commits an error, the Angels of nature are not permitted to interfere with the accompanying compensation men attract in soil erosion and pollution in its many forms. Were the great ones allowed to prevent such catastrophes, we would not learn our lessons concerning the right use and care of the blessings with which nature is endowed.

The Builders of form, unlike the Angels of nature, are not in our atmosphere. The Thoughts of these Architects direct the planning and construction of manifestations that appear as new types of minerals, vegetables, or men. They work entirely from the fifth dimension which is a realm devoted wholly to mental quests.

A colorful group of figures are the glowing Angels of inspiration. Their auras are the shade of flaming sunsets, which contrasts greatly with the contemplative serenity of their faces. Their intense feeling for beauty is expelled in vibrant Thought forms they send earthward. These celestial impressions later appear in actions, prayers and beautiful music. Inspired thoughts are entwined with the imagery of artists and poets so that the ideal might be revealed as a beatitude. These divine dreamers may draw the Spirit of a composer to their fervent levels or they might visit the sanctum of creative effort. The Angels of Inspiration seldom reveal themselves since they concentrate one-pointedly on the flow of lyrical ideas or harmonies reaching an aspiring individual.

The mystic announcement of sunrise sends forth a blessing before which all forms pertaining to the Nature Kingdom, stand expectant. Resplendent colors mingled with the sound effects of the esoteric sunrise vibrate the incantations of the Angels of the morning. They are emissaries from the solar logos, whose task is to direct the spiritual radiation of the sun to this planet revolving before them.

The Celestial Workers who serve us directly and who keep nearer to us than most of the Angelic orders, are the Angels of Love. They are dedicated to the ministry of our guidance, healing, upliftment and harmony. Guardian Angels are beings who devote their time and efforts to our inner unfoldment. We do not attract the attention of these selfless ones until we are consciously seeking God's vast plan and purpose. When our yearning for self-conquest and wisdom grows intense, a Guardian Angel takes her place at our right side. Through her direction, understanding and overshadowing, we are led to the various leaders and teachings we require for our inner training.

A Guardian is of great importance to our higher progress. Next to the Master who is the teacher of our ray, or path, the Guardian Angel stands. Her advice speaks in our intuitions and her teachings speak in our deepening convictions. She leads us into the long corridor of overcoming, and when once within that hall of testing she becomes our examiner and initiator. As time advances us, the Guardian refrains more and more from counseling us. She remains with us during the lengthy process of our inner instructions, but at the first indication of our readiness to think and act independently, she withdraws her influence. Thereafter she remains with us as a protectress, and a compass directing our footsteps. At any time our consciousness is clouded, hers is the clarifying current sweeping the mind of negative debris.

Glossary of Terms
As used in this teaching

Elohim	Sons of God in perfection
Melchizedek Order	Teachers of the soul to facilitate connection of the God Mind to the mental mind; work with the Israel pattern
Israel	Pure pattern of the Son of God; capacity of mental and God minds
God Mind	Seven faculties of mind; God will; Thoughts and Ideas
Mental mind	Five physical senses; man's will; thinking process
Thinking	Processing the information from the five physical senses as personality; processing the reflection from the Thought World
Thought	The perfect pattern which everything comes from; only Heavenly Father creates Thought and man thinks about it through individuality
Idea	Formula that composes Thought
Human being	Has thinking mind that deals only with the five physical senses
Mortal human being	Has God Mind connection and ability of drawing Thought
Nerve Centers (Chakras)	Centers of intelligence that work with God Mind faculties; intelligence behind the working of the glands

Natural	Relates to the spiritual pattern of man; works with individuality
Nature	Relates to the physical pattern of man; works with personality
Earth	Planet we live upon
World	Your own aura or personal universe
Feeling	Consciousness; intelligence; soul
Emotion and Sensation	Mental mind

NOTES

ORDER FORM

To order additional copies of *Mt. Shasta Ascended Master Teaching* or *My Meeting With the Masters On Mount Shasta* if unavailable in your bookstore SEND CHECK OR MONEY ORDER IN U.S. DOLLARS TO SEEKERS AND SERVERS ALONG WITH COMPLETED ORDER FORM TO:

Seekers and Servers
P.O. Box 378
Mt. Shasta, CA 96067

Mt. Shasta Ascended Master Teaching

Quantity   Price

______ X $11.95 = ____________.

CA residents add 7¼ % Tax + ____________.

Total = ____________.

My Meeting With The Masters On Mount Shasta

Quantity   Price

______ X $ 7.95 = ____________.

CA residents add 7¼ % Tax + ____________.

Total = ____________.

ORDER TOTAL = ____________.

Ship to: (Please print clearly)

Name____________________________________.

Address__________________________________.

City_____________________________________.

State________________ Zip Code______________.

KEVIN
LANG
SMITH